Advent Arts
and
Christmas Crafts

PRAYERS AND RITUALS FOR
FAMILY, SCHOOL AND CHURCH

written and illustrated by

Jeanne Heiberg

PAULIST PRESS
New York, N.Y. / Mahwah, N.J.

Acknowledgments

Thanks to my mother, Ruth, for childhood memories of many merry Christmas times; for brother Milton, Aunt Sylvia, Uncle Ken, and cousins Eunice, Beverly, Glen, Judy, and Susan with whom they were shared. Thanks also to Milton for being a great computer teacher and consultant, and to his children, Kim and Eric (with spouses Tom Hogan and Joey), for current shared Christmas joys.

Thanks to Phyllis Farrell for proofreading this manuscript, and to Pam Franzen and her children for being patient models for the cover art.

Thanks to Peggy Linnehan of the Grail Retreat Center, Cornwall-on-the-Hudson, NY, who encouraged and shared good ideas. Thanks to the Grail Movement for deepening my spiritual understanding of Advent and Christmas, and for restoring so many beautiful ways to celebrate. Thanks to Dr. Lydwine Van Kersbergen, Jeanne Plante and Anne Mulkeen for presiding over past meaningful times, and to Trina Paulus, Anne Burke, Ruth Chisholm, Cay Charles, Licia Kraemer, Audrey Schomer, Carolyn Gratton, Alice Gallagher, Ruth Vargas and many others for sharing them.

Thanks to Carol Tomlin, Nellie Brown Bunk, Dee Rincon, Sheila & Roger Lacouture, Carolyne Blake and the Protano family for more recent Advent/Christmas celebrations, and for shared community-building.

Thanks to editor Don Brophy for wisdom, insight and creative élan in guiding this book into print.

Photocopying Guidelines

Library of Congress Cataloging-in-Publication Data

Heiberg, Jeanne.
    Advent arts and Christmas crafts : with prayers and rituals for family, school, and church / written and illustrated by Jeanne Heiberg.
      p. cm.
    ISBN 0-8091-3586-8 (alk. paper)
    1. Christmas decorations. 2. Handicraft. 3. Crèches (Nativity scenes)
    4. Advent calendars. 5. Wreaths—Religious aspects. I. Title.
    TT900.C4H427 1995
    745.594'12—dc20
                                              95-2306
                                                CIP

Published by Paulist Press
997 Macarthur Boulevard
Mahwah, New Jersey 07430

Printed and bound in the
United States of America

Contents

CRÈCHE FIGURES
For cloth Advent calendar pockets
and tree decorations

Cut 2-reverse one

Cut 2 angels - reverse one for other side.

Color, cut out figures, or use as patterns. Make copies to use for different parts.

Basic body, feet, beard, robe, hair, sheep, etc.

for felt: cut all details from felt and glue on basic figure.

Extend trunk to form tab to hold top.

Tab

Cut 2 - one for each side.

Cut extra tree tops for bushes.

Make figures like your family members.

Cut 2 - one for each side.

Introduction

A friend who had made Advent activities a part of family life for years decided the time had come to forgo them. She had started a full-time job, felt exhausted, and after all, her children were older, all in high school now. There was no longer the need there had been when they were little to teach them the meaning of Christmas, and bring them up amid the joys of their Christian heritage.

However, when she announced her decision, she was astonished by the reaction of her children: they were appalled. The sophisticated, blasé bunch became suddenly impassioned, indignant that such beloved and meaningful customs would not be a part of their lives this year. "If you're really too tired, and we can understand that, why don't you let us do them?" they said. And they did.

"I had no idea it meant that much to them or affected them so deeply," she told me. She also wrote about it in a seventies issue of *Marian Helper* magazine, and after our discussion, sent me a copy.

Pat Early's story stayed with me because I also love the customs of the season. I've found that everyone I know who has lived a full Advent and Christmas shares this response. Many are eager to find more ways to help children, and teens too, become more involved in the celebrations and meanings. Arts and crafts, coupled with blessings and celebrations, provide a way. In this book I have taken timeless and traditional modes, added some new ways and meanings and combined them with methods that range from easy to more complex, sophisticated and challenging, to suit different ages, interests and circumstances. There is something to involve everyone in creative expression.

More Involvement Means More Learning

People of all ages do learn and enjoy more when they are involved, and when more of who they are becomes connected to the learning material. Children especially need happy happenings connected with any idea you want to become a major part of their outlook on life. And what is happier than exercising God-given creative capacities in a warm and loving environment, to prepare for a celebration with family and friends?

Religious Education

This is an idea that is, at last, being recognized in religious education where, at least in the classroom, it was too long ignored. Children enthusiastically wielding crayons, scissors and construction paper may bring smiles to adults, but often the question: "How can we waste time on such nonsense when we only have an hour each week to teach them their religion?" But ideas have to be experienced if they are to be a major influence on future thought processes. Connecting crafts to faith adds joy to the learning process, and helps real learning to take place.

At-Home Fun

Fortunately, parents have more than one hour a week with their children. They are in religious education for the long haul, primary imparters of faith, values and Christian tradition.

Teaching at home should be fun, enjoyable for both children and adults. Celebrating the liturgical year, preparing for feasts and holidays has been the traditional and effective way for at-home learning to take place. Even in busy modern households, there is still time to make something together, to say a meal prayer, bless a Christmas tree. What better quality time together?

Community Building

Some of the activities in this book also give ideas for times when many families can get together, support each other as a community, learning and celebrating together. Do not overlook crafts as a way of building community, nurturing faith, and sharing traditions in a happy way.

Visualizing Helps Memory and Making Ideas Your Own

In the early seventies, I gave workshops and evaluations throughout the Albany, New York, diocese in partnership with Mary Reed Newland, author of eight books, and a nationally renowned expert in religious education. When we traveled to Warren and Washington Counties to evaluate catechetical programs, we interviewed young students, as well as their catechists, parents, and parish staff.

Talking with the children was especially instructive. We were struck by how often children remembered from the previous year what was drawn, cut and pasted, acted out, sung, or told as a really good tale. Arts, crafts, puppets, plays, songs and stories made ideas memorable, a more permanent part of a child's memory bank.

A few years later, while listening to a tape on how to improve your memory, I discovered the importance of visual cues. Creating a mental picture will help you retain a memory. In the Middle Ages great effort went into visualizing faith through stained glass, painting, sculpture, and book illumination. In our own time, the biggest budgets for memory-impressing visualizations come from the advertisers.

With colorful, compelling video ads coming at children from all angles, parents and educators need to also employ sight and other senses to teach faith and values. Fortunately, your warm personal presence, offering encouragement and happy experiences, far outweigh what comes from the TV tube. You also have, in catechetics, ideas of real and lasting value that are worth expressing. You and your child(ren) will be rewarded when you share and work together.

Ideas are certainly important in forming faith and values; however, children are able to absorb just so much talk and reading. When you offer ideas, and embody them in happy concrete experiences, learning is far more likely to be internalized.

Tips for Arts and Crafts with Children

As you engage your child(ren) in the crafts, keep their mind(s) in the meanings and the materials, and off the end product. As soon as people of any age start worrying about what their product will look like, they tighten up. They enjoy and learn less, and the product as well as the person suffers.

People and Process Over Product

It's people and process that are important. Grappling with ideas, expressing them through work with their hands, children learn volumes, and produce good things to boot.

If you plan to do the craft with a class or group, it's a good idea to try out the techniques yourself first. One of the gifts we adults receive from children is the good excuse to be creative ourselves, as we plan things for them. Take advantage of that as you use this book. If you are a teacher, do try out the crafts on your own first. No one need ever see the results, but your knowledge and enjoyment will overflow to your children. In the family, you can try things out together, and help each other (your child may help you as well as you them) achieve delightful results.

Whether or not you are pleased by the results doesn't matter; you will not be doing it for an end product, but for the joy and learning that comes with the doing. Keep firmly in mind: *Process and People over Product,* and you will be surprised at how good the products turn out to be.

If you are doing the craft on your own to brighten the Christmas season for yourself, other adults or toddlers, the same principles apply. Enjoy the process and the materials; think about the meanings, and how they are being beautifully embodied in what you do.

Without stirring up worry about how things will look, or focusing on the end product, it's good to encourage care for a craft, and pride in good workmanship. Watch for the time when someone does something well, and point this out, preferably with honest enthusiasm. Create a climate of warmth, encouragement and appreciation. Remember that there are no wrong ways when it comes to arts and crafts; there is only "do your best" and "find your own best way." You can encourage children, and yourself, by saying: "You can't make a mistake in art; there are so many ways to express things, to share ideas visually. Everyone can find their own special way."

Patterns are given in the book to start people off, and to also provide a unity — you can ask people to work in a certain size range, and with matching materials for a crèche, for a sun or star chain, or for decorations. However, many people, once their confidence is raised, will make their own wonderful designs. This is to be encouraged.

Give people all the choices that are practical and possible within the structure of theme, size and materials you set up for a project. They may choose which figure or symbol they will do; how they will interpret it; what color they will use, what details they will add. Tell people to interpret patterns in their own way, and add their own details, touches, decorations where appropriate. Best of all, they should be encouraged to create their own patterns, their own designs. Provide plain white paper or newsprint and pencils for this purpose.

The more of their own vision people put into a project, the more they grapple to express meanings with minds, hearts, hands, and eyes, the more they will be involved. This, and the enjoyment of working together on a meaningful project will help you and others to deepen in faith and in the spirit of Christmas. Gather your materials. Try things out. Share with your people. Learn, and enjoy.

Tips for Blessings and Rituals with Children

Prayer celebrations, blessings and rituals in the family or classroom should be different from those in church. Make them less formal, more fun, involving and, whenever possible, geared to the immediate interests of the people who will take part.

Give children responsibilities, things to do. This can range from carrying a Bible or a baby Jesus figure, to lighting a candle, or reading a prayer or a passage of scripture. The more you involve them, the happier they will feel about this kind of family get-together or class activity.

Ask children, as they are able, to help prepare for a ritual by looking up an appropriate scripture, choosing a song, writing a prayer or poem, and by doing the craft itself.

Use movement when possible, through the house, around the classroom or into the hall and back. Remember that in church liturgies and services, people of different faiths sit, stand, kneel, genuflect, sign themselves with the cross, sing and give verbal responses. The prayer leader in some services gives sweeping gestures, praying with arms raised high, or extended out to the people; children have been known to enjoy some of these. It follows a great tradition; the *Orante*, a female figure with arms raised high was the symbol of the praying church for early Christians. Orante figures have been found in catacombs; they go back a long way.

Some gesture meanings to keep in mind: Arms up express praise and openness, with hands, not clenched into hostile fists, but ready to receive. The Aramaic word for prayer came from *unclenched fist*. Sitting means relaxed, trusting receptivity and listening, while standing says we are ready to take action for God, to do what is right. Processing also says we are joyful in our beliefs, willing to proclaim and live them publicly. Kneeling, bowing, genuflecting, all express wonder, awe, adoration, respect, contrition, asking and requesting. Kneeling before the crèche is a good way to lead children into a moment of stillness before the Christmas mystery. Kissing, hugging and hand shaking are gestures of affection, friendship and support which most children love. They are the external signs, the seal of authenticity on our wish to live out the peace, justice and love of Christ in our lives.

See how different prayer-stances and gestures are received by your young people when you incorporate them into prayer at home or in the classroom. A sure winner is the signing of each child and family member with the sign of the cross on their foreheads, a long-standing tradition both in medieval monasteries, with signing by the abbot/abbess, and in Christian homes, where a parent made the sacramental gesture.

When adults use different actions and sacramental gestures, young minds absorb and retain a great deal. Maria Montessori and Sofia Cavalletti (who developed Montessori's faith development theories) stressed separating word and gesture, to allow the action to speak for itself, in its own time and space. Make the sign of the cross on the forehead in silence; say any words of blessing just before or after. Stop speaking while you light a candle, place a Bible, or bless yourself with holy water.

Gauge the attention span of your group; younger children have shorter attention spans unless they move or do something very interesting. Have a few extra ritual gestures up your sleeve so that you can bring them out when you notice restlessness. Better still, plan variety and movement into the prayer to keep young minds involved. There are many ways to pray, and God loves them all, when they come from the heart.

Use normal times when the family or class gathers to have rituals. In families, meal prayers are a good time for blessings, but keep it short for a hungry group. If you have something wonderful you still want to do, such as blessing the tree, save it for later, perhaps before dessert, when people are fed, mellow and open to ideas. Move to the tree for a blessing, then serve dessert there, to prolong the moment.

Bringing food, fun, and greater involvement to the prayer and ritual is something you can do at home or in a small class. This can feed into and enliven formal prayer times in church, where more decorum is required.

Music and song will also help you to involve children and lead them into prayer. "Advent Song for Children" by Nelly Brown Bunk, is included in this book, in Weekly Advent Wreath Prayers; "Advent Song" by Mary Lu Walker, Paulist Press, is ideal for lighting wreaths. "People Look East" will be enjoyed by children in family prayer. It can be found in the winter edition of *Today's Missal,* issued by *The Oregon*

Catholic Press, Portland, OR., along with traditional Christmas carols and other Advent songs such as: "A Voice Cries Out, Alleluia"; "Hurry the Lord Is Near"; "Christ the Light is Coming"; "Come Emmanuel"; "Comfort My People"; "Maranatha I, II, III"; "On Jordan's Bank"; "Take Comfort, My People", and others. The Catholic Book of Worship issued by the Canadian Catholic Conference, Ottawa, Canada, includes: "O Come, O Come Emmanuel", "O Come Divine Messiah", "On Jordan's Banks", and "Sing Out Earth and Sky". Also adaptable to Advent (and Epiphany) prayer: "They That Wait upon the Lord", "Song of Good News", "King of Kings", and verses one and three of "The King of Glory", found in *Songs of Praise,* Volume 1, Word of Life Communication Center, Notre Dame IN.

Along with moving and singing, ask for moments of quiet stillness and respect during prayers and readings. Peace is one of God's gifts. Setting a magic Advent or Christmas mood with subdued lights, candles, and quiet music will help. If children are restless, try asking them to close their eyes and imagine something beautiful and still — a soft, purring kitten, furry squirrels hibernating in warm dens under white snowdrifts, woolly white sheep asleep on a hillside just before the angels began to shine and sing.

The awe and wonder of the season can help you teach little ones the beauty of stillness. Ask everyone to think for just a few moments about God's love in order to be more open to God's wonderful gifts, including that of joy.

Do encourage the joy that is our gift as God's beloved children. Go with the natural spontaneity of children at prayer; they may surprise you with their responses. The quiet, the joy, the dark, the light, the prayer, ritual, music and crafts together will make the season meaningful and memorable, to nurture people of all ages in their faith.

Advent and Christmas Traditions

The traditions of Advent and Christmas touch hearts in a special way. They speak to all ages, and done well, involve senses, mind, heart and hands in preparations. They form happy memory banks that embody a treasury of meaning. Few ideas follow people through life as well as those embodied in the practices of this season. The crafts, blessings and celebrations in this book are ways to deepen and extend their riches for you, your family, class, or community.

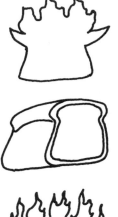

Advent and its wealth of customs help people keep first and foremost the "reason for the season," insuring that Christ be kept in Christmas. A brief history helps to explain this.

The early church celebrated the coming of Jesus on January 6th, the feast of the Epiphany. They were more interested in Jesus' symbolic manifestation to the world as God's Son, and king. It was only in the fourth century that, in the Western church, the birthday became a focal point.

To celebrate this unknown date, the church chose December 25th, when there is the most darkness, and days are shortest. It is right after the winter solstice, when days begin to grow longer, heralding the sun's return in increasing strength. Many cultures celebrated a feast of lights at this darkest time. This meaning was transferred to the Son who came to enlighten, to be the light, to show God's people how to live in light.

This joyful celebration of God's light is the key to the season; however, in early times, there were often too many people to be baptized at Easter, so Epiphany and Christmas also became times to welcome new members into the church. Advent was sometimes seen as a penitential season, a "little Lent." This was reflected in the use of the color purple, but in a rosier hue, for a lighter mood. The season culminates in joyfully welcoming the child, rather than accompanying the man Jesus to the cross.

At the same time (and even earlier), certain segments of the church used dark blue as the Advent color, and this custom has returned. Current church historians, liturgists and other leaders say that Advent is not a penitential season. While either color (or both) may be used, deep blue better expresses Advent as a time of happy waiting and anticipation for the celebration of the light.

Dark blue says it is a time to share stories of our faith and tradition; to remember our spiritual forebears, the Hebrews. Picture them sitting around campfires on cold winter star-spangled nights, keeping alive the stories of God entering their history, promising a better future when the Messiah, the light, will come.

It was a colder and darker time for the human heart before the coming of Jesus into history, and it still is for us, now, when we keep him out of parts of our life. We remind ourselves of this with blue; darkened rooms; candlelight; Jesse tree symbols and Advent wreaths. The Advent emphasis is on expectation and preparation for Christmas, the feast of God's light.

The importance of Advent to our spiritual life has been revived to rescue us from the hectic, fragmenting materialism that threatens to steal away our readiness to welcome God anew each year. The wonderful potential for spiritual growth, for renewal of peace and hope, are too often lost in hectic shopping, rounds of parties, and economic woes. We are too often inundated with superficial and shallow expressions before we have a chance to rediscover the rich meanings embodied in Christmas. Customs from Europe have been renewed to counteract the commercialism that surrounds Christmas.

If we follow the traditions, we will experience Advent as it is meant to be. We will share stories and traditions that draw us together; increase prayer, service and love. We will experience a time of symbolic darkness before the celebration of lights; the longing songs before the joyful carols; the stillness, quiet and simplicity before the exuberance of the Christmas feast.

During the Advent season, it is proper that decorations be subdued, with blue and natural burlap fabrics. Save the bright reds, greens and golds, for Christmas, when jubilation and joy is called for. Keep the house darker in the evenings; turn down the overhead lights in classrooms, at least for prayer and lighting the Advent wreath. The darkness that occurs when humanity is still separate and asleep, awaiting further awakening to God, is a key Advent theme. In a beautiful way, experience a little of the darkness, the longing, as you prepare. Then you can make December 25th a burst of light and joy, rich in the meanings meant for this time.

Christmas becomes more powerful, warm and joyful with the preparation of a well-lived, well-crafted Advent. The crafts and prayers in this book can help you make both seasons beautiful and memorable as you draw people together, and help them deepen in understanding as they enjoy working with their hands.

Frequently Used Techniques and Materials

Because the same materials and techniques are used in more than one craft, information, recipes and steps are given here. You may be referred to them in later chapters. At the end of this section there is also a guide to where materials can be obtained.

Construction (and Other) Paper Techniques

This is a basic material, but typing or copy paper will work in a pinch. Be sure to have a variety of colors. Order mixed colors for family or small group use. For larger groups, if you buy packs separately, order more white, yellow, light blue, red and green; they seem to go more quickly. Besides the primary colors, get light and medium green, blue, pink, lavender, turquoise, purple and magenta, for a full range of expression.

When a project asks you to glue and paste, this means that everything in the design, even the smallest dot for an eye, or a line for a wing or clothing detail is to be cut out of a different color, and pasted down. Young children sometimes need to be told that the design they are pasting is best in a color different from the background, so it will be seen.

Use glue sticks when possible; they are easy to use and clean. A light touch is all that is needed. This is even more true for white glue, which can get messy if used too generously. Protect working surfaces with newspaper and/or plastic.

Glitter

Glitter is great for kids and Christmas, but you have to know how to contain the glitter so that you can also be happy. Fortunately, it's easy and fun.

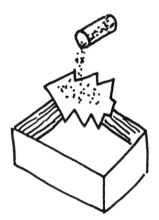

Have only one glitter area or station that people come to as they are ready. Cover it with newspapers or plastic. Have a box or tray, preferably with sides one inch or higher, for each color glitter. Ideally, these should also be larger than whatever will be decorated. The glitter should be the last step in the craft.

To demonstrate the use of glitter:

1. Carefully dribble white glue over your decoration, wherever you want the glitter to stick.

2. Hold it over a glitter catcher (corrugated box, cookie tray, foil dish, etc.), and sprinkle on the color for that box. Keep the colors separated.

3. Shake the excess glitter into the container.

4. Place your decoration carefully on newspaper or plastic to dry.

Magazine Swatches

Paper in many colors, and sometimes in interesting textures, can be had from your favorite magazines. When you are finished reading them, go through them and tear out swatches of different colors, plus black, white, and grey. Look for backgrounds, large cars with big red or blue areas, swaths of sky or grass — you will be surprised at how many and varied the hues. Leave the parts that identify different objects, just go for the color.

As you tear out the colors, you will already have the makings of an interesting collage, with big, medium and little shapes, interesting edges and forms. Combine these with construction paper on collages, figures, and tree decorations.

Cylinder Figures and Features

Cylinder figures are formed by rolling the paper the long way, so that the two longer edges meet in the back, and overlap slightly, where they are stapled. Younger children with tiny hands often need help with stapling. This poses no problem in families, and sometimes two adults or older children with staplers can quickly serve the needs of up to 20 children, 6 or 7 years old.

To give children ideas on how to be creative with their figures, and confidence in what they can do, show them many possibilities. You can draw arms, hair and features directly onto the cylinder, or cut these from separate pieces, and paste them on.

Show the possibilities for taking paper and fringing it, cutting into it at intervals, to form hair, beards, or Native American garb. If the fringe is long enough, it can be curled by drawing it between a child's scissors and your thumb with a little pressure, though not enough to tear it.

Show children how to cut spirals by making a circle, then cutting into it evenly, round and round until you reach the center. Bouncy hair, beards, earrings and decorations of all kinds are the result.

The face may be the cylinder itself, or an oval cut out and pasted on. Eyes may be little football shapes with smaller circles pasted on for pupils, or simply dots, triangles, squares, slits, or any shape you want. Noses also can be a line, a triangle, a triangle shape that is folded to stick out, with tabs for gluing, or it may be eliminated. There must, however, be a mouth.

Everyone knows how to make a crescent moon with upturned corners for a smile, or a small circle, an "O" that shows surprise. Cut a circle or oval in half horizontally, and you have a sweet, sometimes a glamorous mouth, especially if you further form these into lip shapes. A run-through of the possibilities will stimulate imaginations, and help people to discover a full range of ideas.

To add arms, cut out a long, thin rectangle and glue on, or a wider

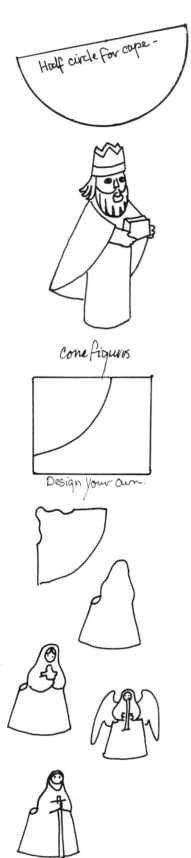

Half circle for cape —

Cone figures

Design your own.

rectangle that you can roll up, for a rounded arm. Cut or add a tab so it can be glued or stapled onto the main body. Some inventive children will form stout legs for their figures with this rolled up method, and keep them standing upright. Children 10 years old and up enjoy this further creative challenge of dimensional forms glued onto the basic cylinder.

To add a cloak, suitable for people in the Bible, place a compass point in the middle of an edge on a sheet of paper and draw a half circle. If you don't have a compass, use a plate. Half the plate should be as long as the cloak you need. Cut out your compass of plate semicircle and form, flat side up, into a cloak that goes around your figure.

Cone People

Figures based on cone shapes are more advanced, a good challenge for older children 9-10 years old and up. Hold a compass point in the corner of a sheet of paper, and sweep the pencil end from one edge of the paper across to the other, in the size you want for a cone figure. Cut out the bottom arc. Draw in the head and arms, then cut out the background shapes behind them. Leave at least two-thirds of the edges, from the bottom up, as they are; don't cut into these. You need these solid edges to join in the back, and staple, for your cone shape.

The cone can be drawn on as is, or added onto with the techniques described above in cylinder figures.

Papier-Mâché

The price is always right for papier-mâché; the main material is old newspapers. Save up your color comic sections so that as you build up layers, you can alternate color with black and white, and keep track of how many layers you have, usually five, and know where one ends and the other begins.

Wallpaper paste is no longer recommended for papier-mâché unless you can be sure it contains no toxins. Your best bet is art paste, officially called methyl cellulose; it's economical, easy to mix and work with, and stores well. A little container will go a long way. If you can't find it in your craft store, you can get it from some of the craft catalogues listed below.

In a pinch, mix flour and water, half and half, as the binder. To add to its adhesiveness, you may want to throw in a little white glue for good measure. The final paste should be like heavy cream. You will also need a mixing container for the paste, and smaller containers if you need to distribute paste to a larger group.

Quick, easy ways to build figures are described later in Christmas crèches. Those made of newspapers can go up to 12 inches, the width of a *New York Times* page. For larger figures, add more layers of newspapers for the base, or other structural devices: crushed foil, wire, and wood structures. You can make life-sized figures with wood and chicken wire armatures if you are ambitious.

Once it is dried, papier-mâché can be sanded, sawed, nailed through, and it is very durable. Painted, it forms attractive, even beautiful figures and forms, and all from old newspapers!

Mash Method Papier-Mâché

You can also make newspaper strips into what is called mash, that can be molded over the previously described papier-mâché, or modeled by itself.

With this method, you need a large pot filled with boiling water, and another pot or box filled with newspaper strips, torn with the grain of the newspaper, then cut into short, 2-inch sections. Drop these into the boiling water just as you would noodles; keep stirring to help the paper fibers to break down. Add a little oil of wintergreen if you wish, to keep a pleasant smell in the mash, especially if it will be stored.

When the paper has disintegrated, pour it through a strainer or colander, and press out excess water with a spoon. Put the pulp in a large plastic container, and add 4 cups of flour or wheat paste for every gallon of mash. This is your basic modeling media. After you have formed your figures, let them dry thoroughly before painting with tempera or acrylics. You can spray them with a clear acrylic sealer after the paint has dried.

If this sounds like a messy project, you are right, but it is fun, creative, and you can make beautiful, durable figures and symbols with it. To make it easier for you, some craft stores and school-supply houses carry a dried mixture that you add water to, mix, and use as you would a home-made mash.

Clay-Dough Recipes

The following are recipes for clay-dough that can be:

1. Rolled out with a rolling pin, thick dowel, or smooth round glass or bottle, then cut into crèche figures, tree symbols, pendants, plaques, etc. Add details and designs by scratching in, or by adding on pieces and pressing them in well.

2. Pressed through a garlic press or pasta maker to form hair, beards, manes on lions and horses, grass, reeds, and any other invention/texture you wish.

3. Molded, like clay, into people, animals, trees, houses, birds, etc. If the dough requires baking, take care that what you make does not vary too greatly in thickness. See instructions in the next section.

Be Sure To Remember To

1. Poke holes through the designs with a toothpick or skewer, if you plan to hang them. For mobile designs that will be placed inside another shape, or contain another shape, be sure to poke holes on the bottom as well as on the top where necessary. Tree decorations, pendants, and plaques need holes for hanging.

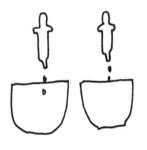

2. Keep a fairly even thickness on forms that will be baked. Create hollow centers by forming a figure around crumpled aluminum foil to hold it upright and/or in place. The foil acts as an armature, and will not be harmed by baking. The foil will also help the inside to cook more quickly.

3. If you wish you can color dough that will air dry by mixing in food coloring liquid or for more vivid colors, the food coloring paste that bakers use.

4. Allow enough time for thorough air-drying before you add color with paint. You may use poster paint, tempera, or acrylic.

5. Make air-drying figures ¼-inch thick, and keep them small. However, you can make them thicker, and build figures up to 4 inches tall around plastic or glass bottles, and microwave them dry. Be sure that there is no metal in the plastic or glass support.

6. For a shiny surface, thoroughly coat the dry, finished works with an acrylic sealant.

Precooked Clay-Dough

    4 cups flour
    2 cups salt
    3 tablespoons salad oil
    1 tablespoon cream of tartar
    2 cups water
    Optional: food color
              paint
              acrylic sealer

Mix flour, salt, cream of tartar and salad oil in a saucepan. Gradually mix in water, and stir over medium heat until mixture thickens, and can be formed into a ball. Remove from the heat, but continue to stir a few minutes longer. When dough has cooled enough to handle, turn out onto a smooth surface. Knead thoroughly until mixture feels elastic, smooth, and holds together well. Use immediately, or wrap well to store in your refrigerator or freezer; this dough keeps well.

It is possible to air dry small objects made from this dough. If you find the objects are not dry after a few days, put them in the microwave for short periods, seconds for small thin objects, minutes for thicker, larger things. You can mend crevices or breaks by smoothing water over surfaces, and pressing soft fresh mixture between breaks, or into cracks. This works until the object is completely dry.

Three Ingredient Baked Clay-Dough

4½ cups flour
1¼ cups salt
1¾ cups warm water
Optional: A teaspoon of alum will help mixture last longer.

Mix flour and salt, then add warm water slowly, mixing it in with your hands. Turn out onto a smooth surface coated with flour and knead until elastic, smooth, and non-sticky; twelve minutes is not too much.

As you form your works of art and artifacts from this dough, it will be important to keep an even thickness. (See instructions above.) Also know that they will puff up slightly during the next step, baking in a home oven.

Bake thin things at 350 degrees for about 30 minutes, larger thicker things at a lower temperature, 325 to 300 degrees, for as long as needed; an hour or more. Keep checking, and if parts are browning too fast while the center is still undone, cover them with foil.

Small and flat things microwave in only 3-7 minutes (don't use foil or anything metallic; cover with waxed paper or a ceramic bowl). They do not brown, but you may prefer the light color as a base for paint.

This dough does not keep as well as the pre-cooked, though you can mix in a small dash of alum, and store in an air-tight container for a while. Your best bet is to make it just before use.

Cooked Corn Clay-Dough With Soda

> 2 parts baking soda
> 1 part cornstarch
> 1 part plus a splash more cold water

Mix dry ingredients, then stir in cold water. Cook over medium heat, until the mixture thickens, about 5 minutes for 8 cups of dough. Remove from heat to cool; cover the pot with a wet towel. When it can be handled, turn out onto waxed paper on a smooth surface to knead for another 5 minutes.

Form works of art and artifacts on pieces of waxed paper, then air dry. When thoroughly dry, paint with tempera or acrylics.

Cooked Clay-Dough With Salt

> 2 parts salt
> 1 part cornstarch
> 1½ parts cold water

Follow the same procedures as for cooked dough with soda. This dough is especially good for rolling out to make ornaments, or for other small freehand designs.

Painting

Many of the crafts call for painting a finished figure or symbol with tempera or acrylic paints. Paints provide the joy of color, and another step in making something beautiful.

Be sure to cover working surfaces with newspapers and/or plastic. When you are working with children, keep jars of paint and water toward the center of the table, where they will not be knocked over by inspired hands and elbows.

Provide young children with basic bright colors, or mix colors for them. Give each color its own brush, so that a child goes from brush to brush, as well as paint jars. Later, teach them to thoroughly rinse a brush in a jar of paint water, and dry it with a paper towel or rag, before they dip it in another color — especially if the next color is yellow or white.

As children grow, provide them with a palette on which they can mix their own colors; an old plate, safe piece of glass with smooth or taped edges, or even an aluminum pie tin will serve. Colors are lightened with white, darkened with black, and grayed with combinations of both. Mixing in a little of the opposite color on the color wheel will also give interesting variations and tones in colors; there is no limit to the interest and beauty that color can provide as mixing skills grow.

Where You Can Get Materials and Supplies

Many projects and patterns in this book can be expressed in paper, fabric, or felt, according to your time, resources, and preferences. Pick up construction paper at a discount store, or substitute typing paper, and keep kids creative and absorbed for 15 to 50 minutes. Visit a fabric/craft shop, or one of the crafts shops that are springing up all over the country. You will find materials that will engross children for hours, days, weeks. Many fabric stores are also expanding their offerings for crafts.

For more specialized materials like art tissue, clay, and art paste, you may need a specialized arts and crafts store or mail order house. Fortunately, current customer interest has brought about more stores, and mail order houses will supply you with everything you need; several, in all sections of the country are listed below. Looking through a good arts and crafts catalogue or store will offer other creative ways of interpreting what you find here.

Dick Blick
Product Information: 1-800-933-2542; to order: 1-800-447-8192; Customer Service: 1-800-723-2787
  East: PO Box 26, Allentown PA 18105, 1-800-345-3042
  Central: P.O. Box 1267, Galesburg, IL 61402, 1-800-447-8192
  West: P.O. Box 521, Henderson NV 89015, 1-800-447-8192

Elementary Specialties
917 Hickory Lane, Mansfield, Ohio 44901-8105, 1-800 292-7891

J.L. Hammett Co.
1 Paliotti Parkway, Lions NY 14489, 1-800-333-4600

Nasco, PO Box 901, Fort Atkins WI 53538, 1-800-558-9595

Chaselle/New England School Supply
P.O. Box 3004, Agawan, MA 01001, 1-800-628-8608, and
9645 Gerwig Lane Columbus MD 21046-1503, 1-800-242-7355

Sax, 1-800-558-6696
P.O. Box 51710 New Berlin, WI 53151
P.O. Box 20511 Lehigh Valley, PA 18002
P.O. Box 5366 Arlington TX 76005
P.O. Box 2837 Rancho Cucamonga, CA 91729

ADVENT WREATH PATTERN
Ages 3 to 8

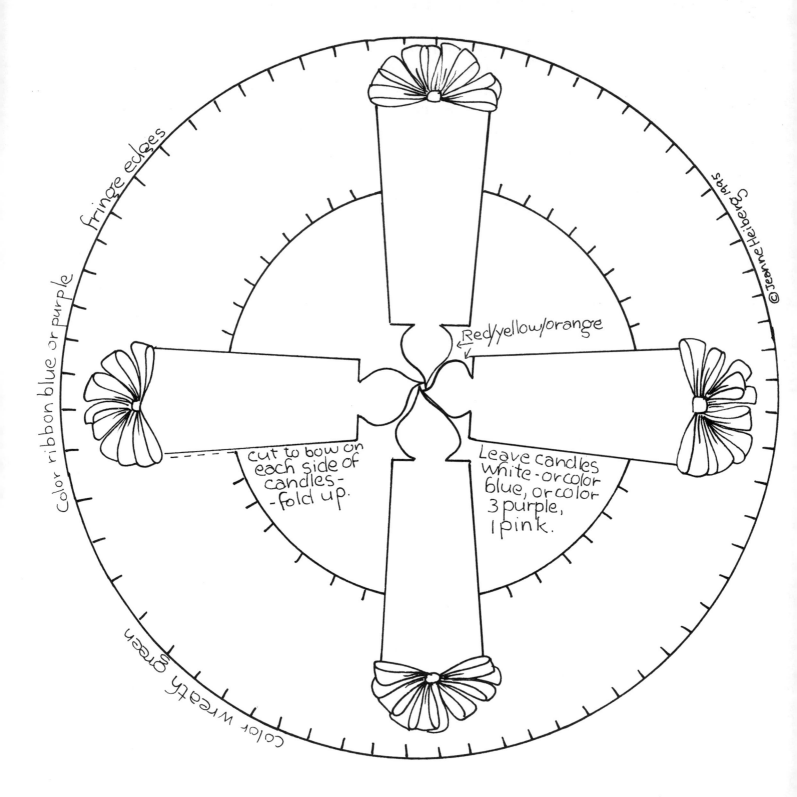

fringe edges

Color ribbon blue or purple

© Jeanne Heiberg 1995

Red/yellow/orange

cut to bow on each side of candles— fold up.

Leave candles white - or color blue, or color 3 purple, 1 pink.

Color wreath green

Advent Wreaths

The Advent wreath, with its green and glowing beauty, carries a message of God's love and involvement in our human history past, present, and future. Its traditional meanings can be expanded with insights from Native Americans. An ideal teaching tool, it's worth spending time on, both in explanation, activity, and prayer. You can combine all three with the first craft, when making the wreath is part of a prayer ritual. Guides follow for quick and easy paper wreaths (don't light the paper candles, of course) so that even very young children can make one in a family, or class.

One large traditional wreath per family or class is recommended as the focal point for Advent prayers. They can be made at home, in class, at a family day (or evening) project, or even during a time of prayer, for a memorable prayer/learning experience. Enough adults must be present for a wreath with real candles, so that their use is well-supervised.

Wreath Meanings

The traditional wreath, wrapped in fragrant evergreens with their fresh, foresty scent, speaks of everlasting life, as does its circle shape. Circles, with no beginning and no end, are a reminder of eternity and, held horizontally (as on a table, rather than vertically, as on a door), speak of our equality before God.

Certain American Indians held the circle as a sacred shape. According to Black Elk, people think of themselves as either on a ladder, or in a circle. On the ladder, other people are either above them, or below them, while in a circle, everyone is equal. Each can look into the eyes of others and see their hurt, pain, need, love, laughter and joy. You need to be in the circle to be at one with your brothers and sisters.

While most of the world knows Black Elk as a Native American of great wisdom, it has recently been discovered that he was also a

Roman Catholic, and a beloved catechist, revered by his people. He successfully integrated Catholic and Indian spirituality, and his wisdom gives the Advent wreath added meaning.

Black Elk's "look them in the eye" view of the circle, as well as European custom, asks that the Advent wreath be hung or set down horizontally, not vertically or slanted. This is also a logical position for the wreath to hold four candles that represent the four weeks of Advent. One candle is lit for the first week, two the second, three the third, and on to the fourth week and Christmas. The increased brightness keeps us looking forward, in happy anticipation, to the celebration of the birth of Jesus, who brought God's light into our dark world.

Not only present weeks of waiting are represented, but also the years his Jewish ancestors longed for Christ's coming. Isaiah prophesied that "those who wait in darkness will see a great light" when the Messiah comes. During Advent, we remember that historical longing, and share it, as the four candles are progressively lit.

The four candles offer another Advent enrichment from American Indians. They saw a sacred sign in the number four as they looked toward the North, East, South and West. Four directions take in the whole world and more: different weathers and moods, possibilities and limitations: warmth, cold, wind, calm, sunrise calls to activity, sunset times for rest.

All of life comes under the sign of four. As each candle of the wreath is lit, it's a good time to pray that God's light and love will be more present to the whole world, all our spaces and times, ups and downs, activities and rests; that all will be illuminated by Christ's light, and come under the reign of God.

In the past, the custom was to have either all white candles, or three purple and one rose for the third Sunday of Advent, called "Rejoice Sunday." Halfway through Advent, the liturgy gives a mini-celebration in anticipation of Christmas. For the youngest children, and for the child in all of us, it's too hard to wait four whole weeks!

The purple candles, and especially ribbons (and if you can find them, berries or dried flowers), should be different from the serious purple of Lent. Advent purple is rosier, more magenta, more joyful than the Lenten color. This season is not so much one of penance as one of expectation, anticipation, and preparation. It is a time to quiet down, to pray and empty yourself of resentments, trivia, and lesser longings to make space for God's tremendous gifts, those that make you really happy. You often hear, during Advent, that the greatest gift is Jesus, bringing God's people into peace, love, hope and joy.

Purple, even rosy, is not the only, or even ideal Advent color; now you may choose blue candles, and blue ribbon, to be changed to red at Christmas, and gold when the feast of the Epiphany celebrates the coming of the wise men to worship the royal infant.

To remove the image of serious penance from Advent practice, liturgists revived the ancient custom of using blue rather than purple as the symbolic color. Either color, or both, now adorn wreaths, vestments, and altar frontals.

A deep blue recalls darkened skies on cold winter nights, when you are more aware of your need for the warmth of God's love, the brightness of God's light. It recalls the ancient tribes of Israel gathered around winter campfires, telling stories of their people, and of the light that will be theirs when the Messiah comes.

Tell stories to your young people also, while their hands are busy making wreaths. Help them take in the riches of Christian traditions, and add a few new practices inspired by Native American meanings. Make Advent a special and beautiful time of prayer and creative learning in preparation for Christmas.

Forming the wreath as part of a family, class or parish prayer is a good way to begin. Briefly discuss the meaning of Advent and wreaths at the learning level of your people. They will absorb more meanings, at a deeper level, during the ritual, because they will be taking part in it. Give the traditional meanings to younger children, and add the newer insights from Black Elk for adults and older children. Prayers to focus on these meanings follow the craft instructions. You can add the ritual action of making the wreath to this prayer, or have a prepared one ready.

Traditional Advent Wreaths

Materials

Advent Wreath base*
4 candles: white, deep blue, or 3 purple and 1 rose

---

* Religious goods stores and catalogues sell metal wreaths with fixed candleholders. Craft stores sell straw and grapevine wreaths into which you can work candleholders or spaces for the bottom of the candle itself.

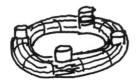

4 FIRM candleholders (ideally part of the wreath base)*

Evergreens, cut small enough to work into wreath. Have at least a
    sprig for all who will be present.

4 ribbon clusters or bows (deep blue, purple, or both)

Florist's (or other thin) wire

Wire cutters or old scissors

Optional: small blue or purple berries

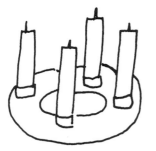

Prayer Needs

A prayer table

A side table to hold all the makings of the Advent wreath

Matches and taper or smaller candle

Optional: A tape player with Advent music
            Prayer sheets and song sheets
            Copies of readings

Functions

Plan ahead how many functions you will need to give everyone present a part in the prayer, and make a list. It may read something like this:

Wreath base carrier	1 (2-3 if very large)
Candles	1-4 (3 if you fix one candle in advance)
Ribbon placer	1-4
Readers & commentators	1-7**
Prayer leader	1
Song leader (optional)	1
Choir (optional)	4-15
Evergreen placers:	1-25 (even more, for an assembly)
Candle lighter	1

For all the kinds of wreaths, anyone who doesn't have one of the roles listed above may be invited to come forward to place an ever-

---

* Scandinavians pushed large nails up into their straw wreaths from the bottom, so that four spikes projected to hold four candles. Some candles have openings at the bottom to accept spike holders. You can also warm the candle bottom to soften it enough to set on the spike. For the ritual making of the wreath, remove the candle, then if possible warm it again slightly just before it will be placed, or have it placed firmly beforehand, and have a child simply present a candle during the commentary.

** Choose children who read well, and give them time to practice. Encourage them to read slowly, and project their voices. If a priest is present, ask him to read and comment on the gospel reading.

green sprig on or around the wreath; have a basket for the overflow, or a very large wreath, great for a sizeable group. Have it carried in by two or three strong young people, who will feel very important. You can also have a huge wreath already in place, hanging or on a table, and eliminate the function of wreath carrier.

For a small family, functions may overlap, and be given informally. The prayer and ritual action can be done in a family of any size, a class, a large group, even a congregation. It will enable all ages to see many meanings in Advent, and welcome the season.

Preparation

For the prayer time, and for the season, keep safety in mind as you prepare; you don't want flames to go any further than the wicks on top of those candles.

If your base is straw, soak it so that it becomes more fireproof, and keeps greens fresher. If you do the forming of the wreath prayer with young children, and have doubts that a child will be able to place candles firmly (don't hesitate to check them even during the ritual), fix the one that will be lit beforehand, and have it standing from the start.

Candle ends sometimes need to be shaved, or expanded with a few strips of aluminum foil to fit a holder. Dripping hot wax into a holder with an old candle, then setting in the new one, helps a candle to be firmly fixed, to insure safety.

Further safety factors:

- Have tall and/or thick candles, so that the flame is kept far from the greens.
- Keep greens from drying out by misting the wreath during Advent, and by keeping the ends wet. Burlap sewn over straw or newspaper, then soaked, allows the evergreen ends, when pushed through, to remain moist. You can also assemble greens in a low bowl such as a quiche dish, circling four candles in holders. Keep a little water in the dish. This makes it easy for people to simply place the greens in a circle during the ritual. Any family or class can do this, and you can remove base, wire and wire cutters from the material list above.
- Another alternative: work a minimum layer of greens onto the wreath so it can be carried in partially prepared. People can add sprigs on top, around, and they can even overflow into a nearby basket.

While safety is a must, don't worry about a perfectly formed wreath during the prayer. You will be able to arrange it for more permanent use later.

To make things as easy as possible for those bringing up the materials, arrange them on a side table in the order they will be picked up. For a large group in a church or assembly, ask a parent to help younger children. Also have a basket of evergreen sprigs at the entrance, so that everyone, especially all the children present, will have one.

Plan for music in the background, and at times when a silent action takes place. A responsible older child or adult can turn it up a little, then down when the reading begins again.

Most of the songs below can be found in *The Catholic Book of Worship* and *Today's Missal;* see *Tips for Blessings and Rituals* in the Introduction to this book. "Advent Song for Children" by Nelly Brown Bunk is included with Weekly Advent Prayers, at the end of this chapter.

Advent Wreath Forming Prayer

SONG: "O Come, O Come Immanuel" or "Advent Song" by Mary Lu Walker

OPENING PRAYER:
LEADER: God of lights, be with us as we prepare, in prayer, for the coming of the true light, Jesus, your Son, whose birth we celebrate at Christmas. Bless each person present, and open our hearts to receive your light more fully. Amen.

LISTENING TO GOD'S WORD
LEADER: Advent is a time to become more quiet, so we can listen to what God says to us in scripture, prayer and life. Let us close our eyes, and listen to God's message in the word, and in Advent signs.
COMMENT: Isaiah, a prophet who lived long ago, said that when the Messiah, the special one sent by God came, the whole world will be able to come into God's light, peace and joy.
FIRST READING: Isaiah 9:1 *(option — half of verse 2)*
READER: The people who were once in darkness have seen a great light; upon those who once lived in the land of gloom, a bright light has shone. You brought them joy in abundance, and great rejoicing.

COMMENT: Jesus' cousin, John the Baptist, was sent by God to point to God's Son, the Messiah, Jesus, so people would recognize him. Sometimes God uses people in our lives to point out God's light and love.

SECOND READING: John 1:6-8

READER: There came a man named John, sent by God, to testify to the light, to point to it. He was not himself the light. The real light, that enlightens every person, was coming into the world.

LEADER: Our prayer today will focus on signs that help us to prepare for the celebration of Jesus' birthday, at Christmas. One by one, the different parts of our Advent wreath will be presented and put together, during our prayer. *(The leader may call each young person by name during the following reading, when it is their turn to present one of the signs.)*

READER: *(May be one, or different for each sign)*

1. The base of the wreath forms a circle. It has no beginning and no end. Jesus came to call us to a life that will never end. *(Reader pauses while wreath base is placed.)*

2. Four candles remind us of the waiting years when the Jewish ancestors of Jesus longed for the Messiah to come and bring God's light into a dark world. They also speak of our own four weeks of Advent-waiting, as we prepare to celebrate Jesus' birth at Christmas. The light will grow week by week, as we welcome Jesus more and more into our lives. Together we can bring more light into this world, so that it is a brighter, happier place. *(Reader pauses as candle(s) are placed or presented.)*

3. Evergreen trees keep their leaves all winter; they don't fall off and die. They remind us that Jesus came to awaken us to the great gift of God: life that will never die no matter how many winters we see. *(Reader pauses while evergreens are placed.)*

4. Blue and purple ribbons remind us to be quiet now, and to let go of some things that are noisy and busy, to make more room for love in our hearts. They remind us to listen to stories of God from the Bible, and to see what stories are created as God works in our own lives,

and the lives of our family members and friends. *(Reader pauses while ribbons are placed.)*

(Optional: include if you have berries, dried flowers or weeds to add):

Other decorations remind us that life becomes more radiant and beautiful, when we prepare times and places to welcome Jesus in prayer, as we are doing now.

LEADER: *(Optional, for a large group):*

As a sign of your willingness to welcome Jesus, and to prepare your heart for his gifts of peace, light and joy, you are invited to come forward to place an evergreen sprig on or beside the wreath. *(Give any further instructions you wish — where to get the sprig, if necessary; order or spontaneity in coming forward.)*

MUSIC: *The ritual may be done in silence, or to quiet meditative taped music to continue during the following meditation.*

MEDITATION

Close your eyes, and imagine yourself in a dark, dark place. It's scary, and so you are relieved and happy when you see a light in the distance. The light comes closer and closer, and you see it is someone you love, carrying a candle.

More candles come, carried by people who love you. Some you know, and some you have never seen before; they come from long ago; they are Bible people.

Everyone surrounds you in light, and someone places a glowing candle in your hands. It is a sign of God's light, love, peace and joy. It is a light you can, if you wish, always carry inside you, in your heart, because Jesus gives it to you. Say a quiet inner "thank you" to Jesus, and to God. . . . Tell God where you need his light in your life right now. If there are any trouble spots, any hurts, wounds, difficulties, tell God about them, and ask God to help.

Thank God again for sending Jesus to light up your life and your world.

Quietly open your eyes, as we light the first candle of the Advent wreath.

(Candle is lit in silence, or to meditative music; there should be no words during this ritual action.)

SONG: "Advent Song for Children" by Nelly Brown Bunk or "On Jordan's Bank"

CLOSING PRAYER

        Jesus, you are the true light, come to awaken a dark world to the love, peace and joy that God meant us to have when we were created. Help us to awaken more fully to your presence. May our Advent preparation and our Christmas celebration bring more happiness to each of us, and to our world. Amen

SONG: "Sing Out Earth and Sky," or "Christ the Light is Coming," or another verse of "O Come, O Come Immanuel."

Wreaths With Native American Meanings

· FOR AGES 9-12 ·

Materials

    Glue sticks or glue
Scissors
Construction paper, 9″ × 12″: white, green, blue and purple
Construction paper scraps, or pieces cut 3″ × 4″ or smaller.

Preparation

    Have all the materials on a table where they can be easily picked up or distributed.

Developing the Craft

    Cut the components out of construction paper, and assemble them according to instructions on the sheets. Encourage young people to make their own choice of colors for candles and ribbon, after explaining the meanings of each. Tell them, if they wish, each candle and corner can represent North, East, South and West, to pray for Christ's light and love to come to the whole world. They may put Indian designs on sections of the wreath, the candle, or the ribbon to express this.

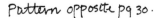

Pattern opposite pg 30.

· FOR AGES 4-8 ·

Materials

Copies of wreath pattern (should be precut for 4-5)
Glue sticks or glue
Magic markers and crayons
Scissors for older students

Developing the Craft

1. Distribute patterns, precut for younger children not yet adept with scissors. Those who can, cut out wreath, candles, ribbons and direction signs.

2. Children draw and color leaves, bows, add their own Native American designs.

3. Cut sides of candles to bows; put a crease in them so they will stand up. Fasten with tape if necessary.

Native American Advent Wreath Prayers

PREPARATION

Gather, and have ready: a pre-made traditional Advent wreath, either a paper symbolic wreath, or a full, traditional wreath as described earlier. Add, if available, and in Advent colors, some of the following: Indian beads, feathers, symbols of four directions (North, East, South, West); an American Indian, Mexican, or Southwestern covering for the prayer table. Some stoles have bold, Indian-like bands of color. If a priest presides, ask him to wear it.

Place the Advent wreath and the prayer table in the center of an open space, so that everyone can stand around it in a circle. Have matches handy. Prepare songs or recorded music, and include other prayers from this chapter if you wish.

THE PRAYER:

Invite all present to stand in a circle with the wreath at the center.

LEADER: Jesus said, "Father, that they all may be one, as I am in you, and you are in me. May they be one in us."
            (Ask someone present to light the correct number of candles for the current week in Advent)

LEADER: The circle shape of our Advent wreath helps us to understand the oneness that Jesus calls us to. Even though some of us are taller, some smaller, in the circle we can take one another's hands, and look into one another's eyes, bless one another, and help one another. Let us (hold hands now as we)* pray:

PRAYER: Great Father, may we be one family in you; may we care for and help one another as we prepare to celebrate the birth of Jesus. He came to bring us light, and make us one in you. Help us see each other as your sons and daughters, loved, and made loving by you.

RITUAL ACTION

LEADER: Turn to the person beside you, look into his/her eyes, and see that person as God's beloved son or daughter. Now turn to the person on the other side of you, and see that also. Close your eyes, and feel God's great love all around you. God loves you very much, and wants you to share that love with others.

Open your eyes, and ... *(sing a song, go quietly to your seats — give instructions for the next phase of activity).*

Weekly Advent Wreath Prayers

Play Advent music from a cassette, and/or sing favorite Advent songs; add readings and prayers from the Sunday lectionary, if you wish, as enrichments. The scriptures below are given as added resources. For young children, and at meal prayers, you may want to simplify, and say only the prayers.

First Week
(Isaiah 63:16-17, 19; 64:2-7; 1 Corinthians 1:3-9; Mark 13:33-37)

Loving God, we light this candle as we prepare for the celebration of your Son's birth on earth. Help us to further "wake up" to you during this Advent season. As we welcome Jesus, let love be renewed and strengthened in our hearts, in our minds, and in all our actions. Amen. *(Light one candle.)*

---

* If you think a group of older children ages 9, 10 and up will be too self-conscious or silly when you ask them to join hands, you may want to skip this gesture.

Second Week
(Isaiah 40:1-5, 9-11; 2 Peter 3:8-14; Mark 1:1-8)

Lord God of light, you have baptized each of us into your family, in Jesus your Son, whose coming we prepare to celebrate. During this holy season, may we empty our hearts and minds of selfish and small aims, so that you may fill us further with your light. We celebrate your presence in each other, and serve each other as we wait. Amen. *(Light two candles.)*

Third Week
(Genesis 3:9-15, 20; Ephesians 1:3-6, 11-12; Luke 1:26-38)

Lord God of light, it is in your love that we find lasting joy. Through prayer and kind service, may we prepare ourselves for the gifts of peace and joy you want to give us. Help us to "make up" with one another by forgiving when we feel hurt or angry, so that we may be happy together in Jesus, through whom we pray. Amen. *(Light three candles.)*

Fourth Week
(Isaiah 6:1-2, 10-11; 1 Thessalonians 5:16-24; John 1:6-8, 19-28)

Lord God of light, you sent your Son, Jesus, to be like a sun that always shines, that no darkness can put out. May the light of Jesus' peace, love and joy be bright in us, and may we generously share this light with others in kindness and helpful service. Amen. *(Light four candles.)*

"Advent Song for Children" by Nelly Brown Bunk

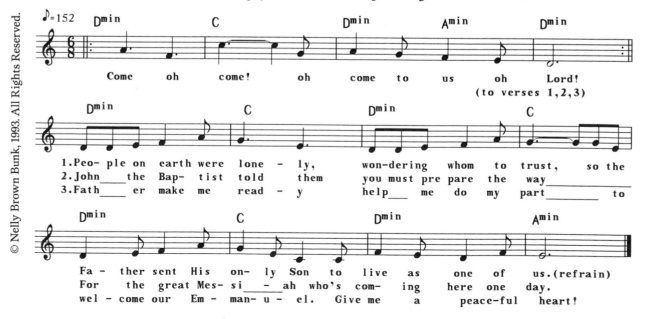

ADVENT WREATH PATTERN
Ages 9 and up

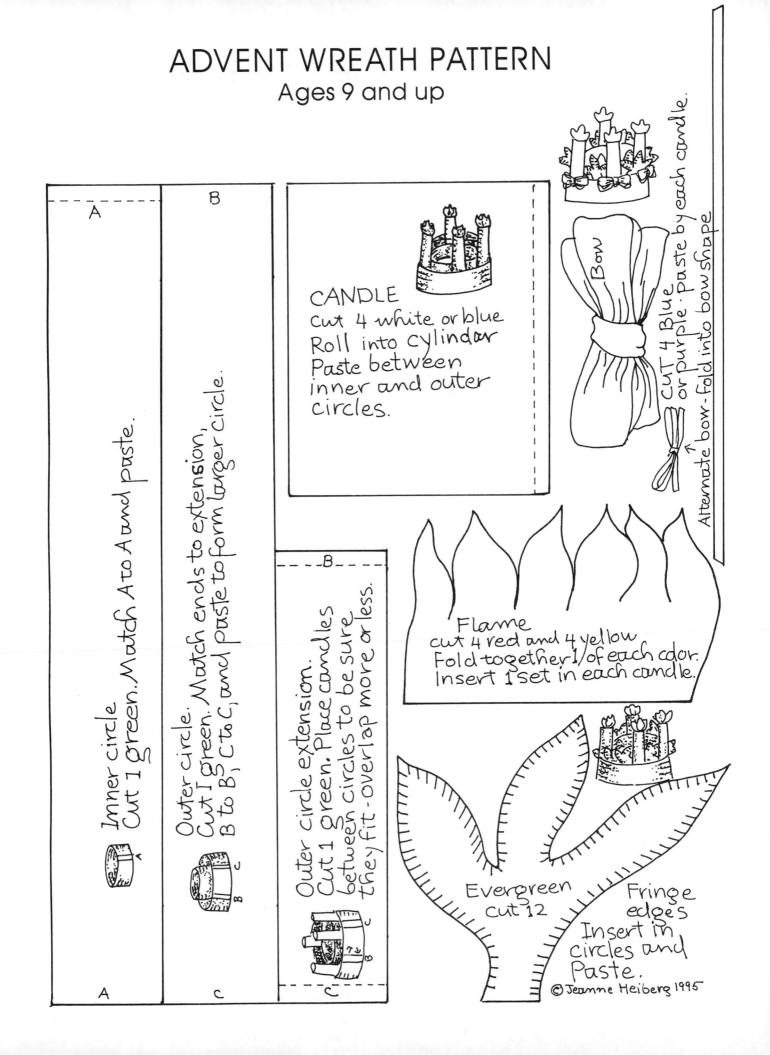

A

B

Inner circle
Cut 1 green. Match A to A and paste.

Outer circle.
Cut 1 green. Match ends to extension,
B to B, C to C, and paste to form larger circle.

Outer circle extension.
Cut 1 green. Place candles
between circles to be sure
they fit - overlap more or less.

CANDLE
Cut 4 white or blue
Roll into cylindar
Paste between
inner and outer
circles.

Bow

Cut 4 Blue
or purple. Paste by each candle.

Alternate bow - Fold into bow shape

Flame
Cut 4 red and 4 yellow
Fold together 1 of each color.
Insert 1 set in each candle.

Evergreen
Cut 12

Fringe
edges
Insert in
circles and
Paste.

©Jeanne Heiberg 1995

ADVENT CALENDAR

Advent Calendars

Children look forward to Christmas; small ones, especially, can hardly wait. To help them wait as you teach faith meanings, make and use Advent calendars.

A simple paper calendar is included for you to copy for older children to make and use; the cutting is complex for very small hands. Younger children 3-5 years old may enjoy coloring it, or pasting pieces of old Christmas cards inside, but they will need your help cutting out the windows. You may want to prepare the entire inside so that they will have a surprise each day.

Instructions for a cloth Advent calendar follow here, with 24 pockets, each to contain a discovery, a treasure for each day leading up to Christmas. This is for an adult to make for small children, 3 years old and up. You have a choice of what to put in the pockets: found objects, sewn symbols, words/pictures cut from old cards, or things hand-drawn and written. To make the calendar more meaningful in relation to Christmas, place the makings of a Christmas crèche in each pocket; small figures are pictured on page iv, opposite page 1. Use a copy machine to reduce or enlarge them to fit your pockets. If you do it in paper or felt, large pieces such as the stable can be folded or rolled up to fit a pocket.

Patterns and ideas from the Jesse and Christmas tree decorations will also provide many ideas that you can reduce in size. You may want to add symbols that relate to family events and your child's experiences.

33

Paper Advent Calendar

· FOR AGES 6 AND UP ·

Materials

> Advent calendar copies
> Crayons and markers
> Scissors and glue stick
> Optional: old Christmas cards, copies of diocesan newspapers, religious and other magazines that relate to the spiritual side of Christmas.

to copy and color:
Paper calendar
opposite page 31.
Backing Sheet
opposite page 39.

doors open to show backing.

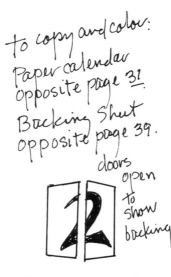

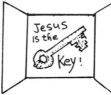

A new picture and message – every day!

Initiating the Craft

Tell your child that Advent is a time to prepare for a great celebration that everyone loves — Christmas! We do things to get ready for Jesus' coming now, to us and our world. We all need the peace, love and joy of God that he brings. Because we celebrate this at Christmas, it becomes a happy time.

The Advent calendar is a way of marking the days in anticipation, and preparing our minds and hearts to be open and receptive to God's love. Opening new doors or finding new treasures in pockets each day will be fun, and our joy in God and Jesus will grow.

Developing the Craft

1. Prepare the front of the calendar, the one with the house, by coloring it, and cutting open the windows on the dotted lines.

2. Prepare the second sheet of the calendar by coloring in the windows, making your own drawings to paste in, or by adding words and designs from old Christmas cards, magazines and newspapers.

3. Turn the front sheet over, and run a glue stick around the edges, about one inch in. Turn it face up, and carefully place it over the second sheet, so that the edges match, and it lies smoothly.

4. Post the finished calendar on the refrigerator door, on a bulletin board, or in your child's room.

Cloth Calendar

· TO MAKE FOR CHILDREN ·

Materials

Suggested colors for calendar front, pockets, and pocket linings: two or more calico prints in shades of blue and purple, or in reds and greens. Try a deep blue or turquoise calico background with purple or plum calico for pockets, with solid colors for borders. To make a background for felt crèche figures, add a felt panel in dark blue (for a blue/purple color scheme) or

EASY ALTERNATIVE A: Make the entire banner out of felt. With no need for a seam allowance, cut the pockets slightly smaller, and eliminate linings. A felt calendar can be easily stitched by machine, hand, or glued together. Felt provides a temporary flannel board for crèche figures drawn out of pockets day-by-day. A child can place them easily. Later, you can pin them from the back to stay up for the season.

EASY ALTERNATIVE B: Instead of individual pockets, make six long strips, 2½" × 17" for each row. Also cut backings and stitch to the first strips on three sides, both with wrong side out. Turn inside out, press, and turn in the remaining seam. Place these in rows down the calendar, and stitch the bottoms, ends, and at intervals to form 4 pockets equal in size.

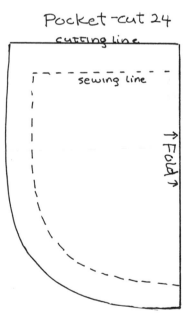

Pocket - cut 24
cutting line
sewing line
↑Fold↑

Also for lining - cut 24

Cloth and Other Materials

1 yard for front. Cut out a piece 24" wide by 36" long.
1 yard for backing. Cut out a piece 24" wide, but leave the length to be cut later.
¼ yard for pockets. Cut out 24.
¼ yard for pocket linings. Cut out 24.
Two ¼-yard pieces, solid colors that match prints.
Bright yellow, gold, and other color scraps.
Iron-on mending tape/patches, or felt for numbers, or, dates 1-24 cut from an old calendar.
Scissors, pins, needles and thread to match cloth.
White construction paper, pencil, chalk and ruler.
Sewing machine and/or thimble or fabric glue.

Options

A felt panel, 9″ × 16″ to create a temporary flannel board.

Multicolor felt scraps for crèche figures, or 24 small treasures or favors to go in the pockets (favors, toys, Jesse tree symbols, old Christmas card pictures), or, figures from this book copied and cut out, or made from construction paper, felt or clay dough (see recipes at the end of the introduction to this book).

Extra trims, ribbons, rickracks, cloth strips, buttons, bells, etc. to add more color and design.

Developing the Craft

Cut out both the calendar and its backing to measure 24 inches wide by 34 inches long. Cut out 24 pocket shapes and 24 linings in a contrasting print or color.

Pin pocket fronts and linings face-to-face, wrong side out, and stitch around the edges, except for a 1½-inch space on the top or side — a straight edge. Clip the corners, and turn the pockets right side out, so that seams are hidden. Press, and stitch up openings.

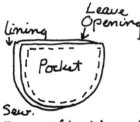

Sew or glue numbers 1-24 (cut from felt or old calendar) onto pocket fronts, or cut from mending patches and iron on.

Arrange and pin pockets evenly in rows 4 across and 6 down, beginning with number 1 at the bottom left, and ending with 24 at the top right. Leave 10 inches at the top for December 25th, or as much space as you will need for a large star/sun, or small nativity scene. Sew the pockets to the calendar front.

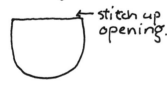

December 25th

This date must be a climax at the top. If you plan a star, sew it on now. If you wish, add rays (cut felt lines, rickrack etc.), and any other trim, ribbon, decoration you wish.

If you plan a crèche formed by figures drawn out of the pockets each day, leave enough space for the scene. You may want to iron, glue or sew on small velcro pieces where the figures will go, so they can be easily and ceremonially attached later. With a felt panel, felt or sandpaper-backed paper, figures will adhere for awhile after they are placed, and you can pin them from the back later.

Place the felt panel so that the top is flush with the rough edges of the calender, and the rest hangs down toward the pockets.

Optional Borders and Hanging Tabs

Cut two bands 24″ × 2″ from a solid color to form borders to frame the top and bottom. Place one face-to-face with the bottom of the calendar, the other with the top, over the panel, so that all the edges are even. Sew each ½ inch in from the edge, then open, so that they form an extension of the calendar, lengthening it. Repeat this for the top of the calendar. Cut two more 24″ × 4″ bands in a contrasting color for a backing to these strips, and set aside.

Cut five hanging tabs, 3½″ × 7″ long, and contrasting linings the same size, from solid colors that match your calicos (blue and purple, or red and green, etc.). Each tab is made up of two pieces of material, both about 4 inches wide by 6 inches long. Place them face-to-face, and stitch up the sides. Turn them rightside out, press, and bring both rough ends together to form a loop. Place these ends at the top of the banner, loop end down, with the raw edges against the raw edge of the framing strip. Place one framing strip backing over the loops, exactly in place with the first framing strip, and carefully pin and baste. Turn right side out so that loops are at the top of the calendar. You may want to arrange the contrasting lining so that a narrow portion shows behind the loops. Pass a dowel or stick through the loops, and see how the banner will hang. Make corrections, then turn back to the raw edges, and sew by machine. Turn right side out again, and press.

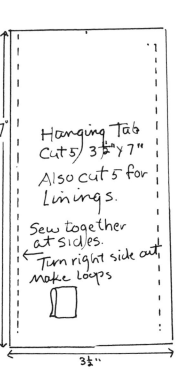

Make five framing tabs, 4 inches wide, 7 inches long, cut to form a V at the bottom. Cut identical linings. Place the tabs and linings face-to-face, and stitch the sides and the V at the bottom, leaving only the top open. Turn the tabs right side out and press.

Place the tabs on the calendar with the V pointing up, and the top, raw ends of the tabs pointng down, and even with the raw edge of the calendar bottom. Place the second contrasting framing strip over this, and sew as described above for the loops. The tabs should hang down at the bottom of the calendar.

Cut the backing cloth to the same length as the front, and place them face-to-face. Sew together on both sides. Turn right side out, and press. Tuck the raw edges on the back under the back framing strips; also tuck in all the framing strips on the sides, and on the back, and hem by hand.

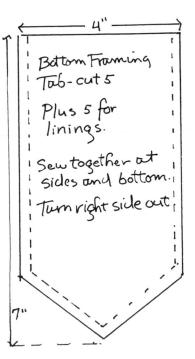

Pass a stick or dowel through the loops, and tie a piece of string or yarn to both ends for hanging.

For the Pockets

A. Look for small favors and items that will be surprises, treasures, for children, or choose ideas from other chapters in this book, reducing or enlarging patterns to fit the pockets.

B. Make crèche figures for each pocket: the stable, a hay manger for Mary and another for Jesus, and trees. Progress to sheep, doves, donkey, shepherds, angels, star, then figures from your own family. For the last three days add Joseph, Mary, the baby Jesus. Use the pictures included here as is, or interpret them in construction paper, felt, or even cloth with raw edges held by fabric glue.

Variations

Change the size of the calendar to match your wall space, and the size of pocket contents; use a copier to reduce or enlarge.

Add a symbol or decorative shape to the hanging loops and bottom tabs. Add more framing strips to the top and bottom, and/or sides, or eliminate them entirely for simplicity. You can also skip the hanging tabs and loops and hang with push-pins.

· OLDER CHILDREN AND TEENS ·

Many older children and teens will also enjoy a pocket cloth calendar with crèche figures; however, you can also insert slips of paper with words: fun and challenging things to do, loving, affirming messages, scripture, or "thoughts for the day."

Old cards, parish bulletins, diocesan newspapers, spiritual-reading books, religious magazines, children's religion textbooks and daily devotional books will supply the inspiration and ideas you need to carry out this custom for many years.

Follow-Up Activities

Open the doors of the Advent calendar day-by-day, or reach into a pocket to draw out a crèche figure or other treasure. There may be more or fewer days than 24. For more, wait until December 1 to start. For fewer days, empty two pockets or more close to Christmas.

Try to have this ritual at the same time each day: with the meal prayer, at bed time (for the next day), afternoon snack, or when school children or Daddy comes home. If you wish to include prayer as a part of this event, use some that follow, or make up your own to relate to your child's experiences and needs.

FOR CLASSROOM AND CHURCH USE: Build a crèche weekly; have several children come forward and empty pockets for the next seven days. Have the crèche figures barely peeping from the pockets to stir up anticipation.

Advent Calendar Prayers

1. Jesus, we look forward to the celebration of your coming at Christmas. Give us patience as we wait and prepare for that day. Open us to your love, and to all the gifts you bring. Amen.

2. Jesus, we can hardly wait until your birthday comes. The joy of that day is just a little taste of all the happiness you want for us, as you bring us God's peace and love. Amen.

3. Help us, our friend Jesus, to prepare our minds and hearts to receive you and your gifts of God's peace and love at Christmas. Be with us, to bless each family (class) member and friend to be ready for your great day.

4. Gentle and loving Lord Jesus, the days are dark and cold outside, but the thought of your love warms our hearts and makes us glow. We look forward to the happiness of celebrating your birthday soon. Help us, through our prayers and acts of love, to be a little more ready each day.

5. Bless our family, Lord, that your love in each of us may grow day-by-day, as we prepare to celebrate your coming at Christmas.

6. Loving God, we look forward to opening our Christmas gifts, but help us to realize that the greatest gift is Jesus, your Son, who teaches us how to love you and one another. May we see the love behind each gift we receive, and let you make a gift of us to others, in the love we give.

7. Jesus, may each surprise we take out of each pocket help us to remember what and who we are getting ready to celebrate: you, and your coming to us. Help us to be alert for all the times you surprise us with your love, and help us to surprise others as we share your love with them.

ADVENT CALENDAR BACKING

Color, if you wish, then paste in back of calendar so pictures
will show through windows as they are opened during Advent.

JESSE SYMBOLS
Ages 3–8

Elijah

color, cut
paste on light
cardboard.

Use out lines
to make your
own designs.

Lion
of
Judah

Moses

Isaiah

Jacob

Ruth

Rachael

© Jeanne Heiberg 1995

TREE SYMBOLS

To cut from construction paper or two pieces of felt- sew and stuff. Cut and glue details in different colors.

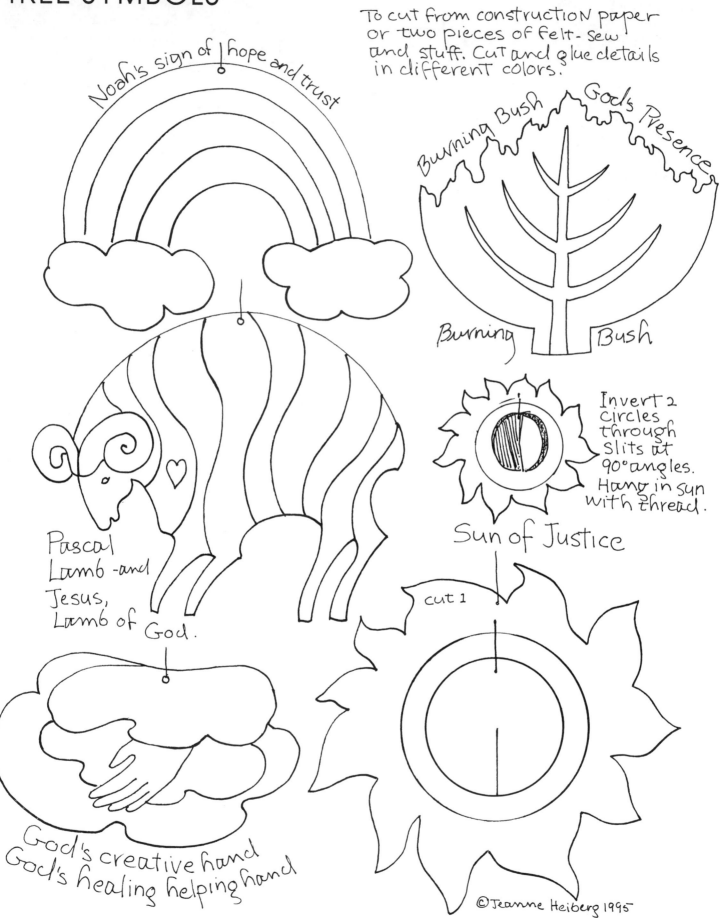

Noah's sign of hope and trust

Burning Bush   God's Presence

Burning   Bush

Pascal Lamb -and Jesus, Lamb of God.

Invert 2 circles through slits at 90° angles. Hang in sun with thread.

Sun of Justice

cut 1

God's creative hand
God's healing helping hand

Tree Decorations

FOR ADVENT AND CHRISTMAS

The lighted decorated Christmas tree, a treat for all, speaks volumes of meaning. Evergreens say that Jesus came to welcome us into a life that will never end. The lights remind us that he came into a dark world to bring truth, enLIGHTenment, and the brightness of God's presence.

Colorful, shiny, delightful decorations tell of the joy Jesus shares, that brings us to awareness that we are God's beloved sons and daughters, family members all. Let the making and hanging of ornaments be a reminder of this call to joy.

Many decorations have further meaning. Jesse tree symbols recall the centuries of Hebrew preparation for Jesus' coming. A flower sprouts from the root of Jesse, family forebear of Jesus, along with King David, symbolized by a star, key or crown. Jacob's ladder, Joseph's coat of many colors, and the lion of Judah also relate to ancestry. The ram that replaced Isaac in sacrifice, and the paschal lamb prefigure Jesus' sacrifice. Noah's ark or rainbow and Jonah in the whale are lighthearted reminders to trust in God, while the apple, minus a juicy bite, celebrates the "happy fault" of Adam that merited so great a redeemer. Tents tell of the Israelite's trek through the desert carrying the tabernacle, sign of God's presence among the people. Now we find this presence in Jesus, and in those who receive him hospitably into their own "tent" of body, mind and heart. A Sun of Justice remembers prophets who spoke about the coming Messiah, the better world he would bring, and our own call to help form it in a holy and creative partnership.

Other symbols speak of what happened after Jesus' birth. Decorated globes say he came to save the whole world, and the whole of us. Circles and globes also speak of eternity, and many people brought into unity. Stars and doves tell us of hope, and of the special guide we have in the Holy Spirit. Hearts remind us of God's love, and the love God wants us to extend to others. Birds speak of the mustard seed tree of

Jacob

Isaiah

faith; bells ring out the good news; lanterns and candles say "Jesus is the light of the world." Every other decoration declares Jesus' wish to bring joy to every aspect of our lives. He wants us to be happy, and to help each other to be happy, as we must be when we know that, in him, we are empowered to be people of the light.

As part of your Christmas preparations, make some of your own ornaments this year. Use them to decorate the family tree. Hang Jesse tree symbols early, but save the rest until Christmas Eve. When the tree is trimmed, use the *Christmas Tree Blessing* as a transition from Advent into Christmas. And may God bless not only your tree, but you, your family, and friends.

Some Ways to Approach Tree Decoration Projects

Making tree decorations is an ideal project for the month of December, and it can take many forms, fill many needs. By making use of the resources in this book, the following people can accomplish the following goals:

- PARENTS: Fulfill your parental role as primary teachers of religion to your children, and transmit important values, as you have fun with them. What better quality time?
- CATECHISTS: Help your children celebrate and learn more about Old Testament roots, and New Testament fulfillments.
- PARISH LEADERS: Help your parish to build community by bringing together people of all ages and states in life for a joyful and meaningful experience.

The Christmas tree meanings outlined here, sometimes with added time, date, and place, sometimes on the reverse side of the *Christmas Tree Blessing* (at the end of this chapter), has served all these groups. Some of the ways they have been used follow, to give you inspiration for your Advent programs:

1. Parents used the letter to learn more about the meanings of Jesse tree symbols and Christmas tree decorations to talk about them to their children, and enrich the faith life of the family.

2. Older children were given the letter to study, and look up scripture verses and stories to share at a meal prayer, Advent wreath lighting, or blessing of the Christmas tree.

3. Directors of religious education and catechists sent home the letter with the *Christmas Tree Blessing* on the reverse side, to support parents in their role as primary religious educators of their children.

Patterns and ideas for making decorations sometimes accompanied the letter, ranging from simple to complex for different age levels.

4. Parents who received the letter said they and their children had fun doing things together; the *Christmas Tree Blessing* provided added meaning to their celebration, and supported the faith life of the home, the "little church."

5. Catechists used the letter as a basis for discussing meanings and making decorations for a class tree. The blessing was prayed in class. Copies of the blessing were decorated with crayons or markers as a class project, and taken home to encourage family prayer.

6. The letter was inserted in a parish bulletin, with an invitation to everyone to come to the community room after a popular mass to enjoy refreshments, listen to music, and make decorations together. Someone remarked: "There wasn't a face without a smile." Practical ideas for making this a success follow under "Community Building."

7. Parents in a Saturday religion program were invited to come twenty minutes early to pick up their children (who previously took home the letter) on the last session before Christmas. A celebration with procession, prayer and song preceded the community building decoration project and the refreshments. This is described in the last section of this chapter.

These ideas may inspire you to build up old and new traditions that call forth creativity and prayer in your home, class or parish.

"Initiating The Craft" has been skipped in the instructions that follow. Discussing the meanings, showing the materials, playing Advent and Christmas music is usually enough to get things going for faith-filled learning and fun. Use the letter, the *Jesse Tree Chart*, and the scripture references in combination with the craft to build happy memory banks and help your children in their growth as young Christians.

Moses

Jesse Tree Symbols

· FOR AGE FOUR AND UP ·

Materials

Multicolored construction paper or light cardboard*
Scissors and optional hole punch

Rachael

---

* Felt, an added option, may be pasted over tagboard, light cardboard, or cut in two pieces, sewn and stuffed (add needles, thread, tagboard or cotton to your list).

Glue stick, glue, stapler and staples
String or yarn
Pencils, magic markers and crayons
Newspapers and/or plastic coverings to protect work surfaces
Optional: Patterns and Jesse tree chart copies
            Evergreen tree, or beautiful bare branches, for samples,
            and for hanging as works are completed.

Preparation

For an at-home project: assemble the materials, prepare some
cocoa and cookies, put on some Advent music, and begin. You can help
small hands cut and paste as you go, and from time to time, explain the
meaning of a symbol, and why we decorate Christmas trees. You are
helping your child(ren) to build firm faith foundations as you combine
meanings and activities in this way.

For classes: Pre-K and K-2 teachers may want to have symbols
precut, or have some guest parents on hand to help those who have dif-
ficulty in cutting. Even for those who cut well, you may want to prepare oak tag or light cardboard templates for people to use as tracing
guides.

You may also want to set up a tape player with Advent music, and
a small evergreen tree or beautiful bare branches for samples, and/or
the complete work of your young people.

For parishes or larger community groups, see the last section in
this chapter.

Developing the Craft

1. Look at the *Jesse Tree Chart* and its symbols, to choose the symbols you and your child(ren) want to work with. Talking about the
ancestors of Jesus while you choose will help to extend their faith
awareness. Also provide this choice: "You may create your own symbol,
drawing your own pattern or template on white paper or tagboard, or
use one of the patterns in this book. If you use a pattern, add your own
creative touch."

2. Cut the symbol out of construction paper, using your own design, one of those provided, or a template as a guide. Place a template on
the paper, trace around it, and cut. With a paper pattern, you may cut
roughly around the symbol, place it on the construction paper, and
hold in place with scotch tape. Cut through both pattern and construction paper together, using the outline as a guide.

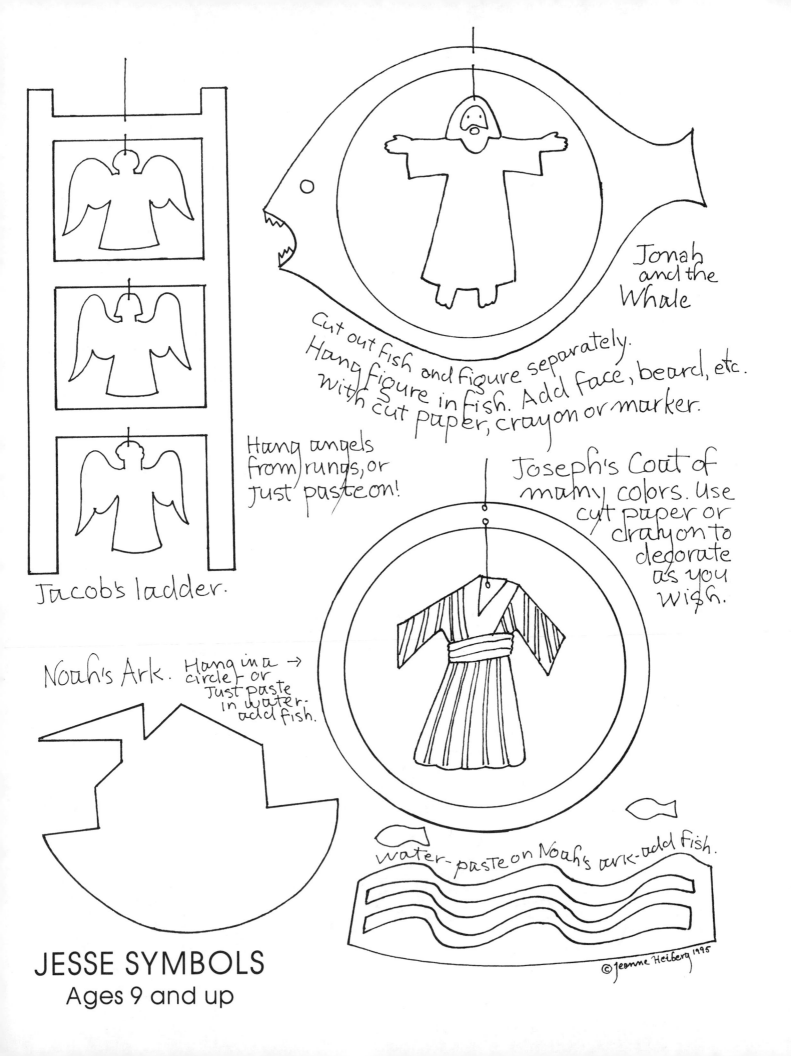

Jonah and the Whale

Cut out fish and figure separately. Hang figure in fish. Add face, beard, etc. with cut paper, crayon or marker.

Hang angels from rungs, or Just paste on!

Jacob's ladder.

Joseph's Coat of many colors. Use cut paper or crayon to decorate as you wish.

Noah's Ark. Hang in a circle or Just paste in water. add fish.

water-paste on Noah's ark-add fish.

©Jeanne Heiberg 1995

JESSE SYMBOLS
Ages 9 and up

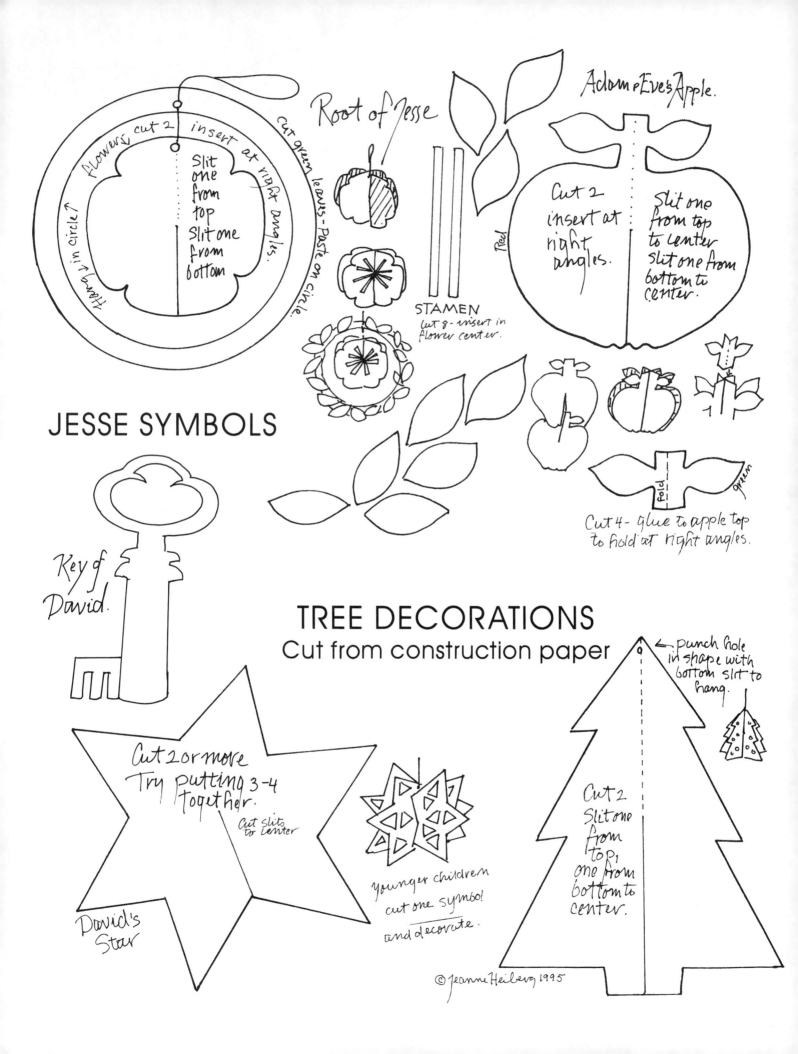

Flowers cut 2 insert at right angles.

Hang in circle?

Slit one from top slit one from bottom

cut green leaves - Paste on circle.

Root of Jesse

Adam & Eve's Apple.

Red

Cut 2 insert at right angles.

Slit one from top to center slit one from bottom to center.

STAMEN
Cut 8 - insert in flower center.

fold

green

Cut 4 - glue to apple top to hold at right angles.

JESSE SYMBOLS

Key of David.

TREE DECORATIONS
Cut from construction paper

← punch hole in shape with bottom slit to hang.

Cut 2 or more Try putting 3-4 together.

Cut slits to center

Cut 2 Slit one from top, one from bottom to center.

David's Star

younger children cut one symbol and decorate.

© Jeanne Heiberg 1995

3. Add features, robes, or any other decorations by:

    A. Drawing with marker or crayon, or

    B. Cutting them out of construction paper (in colors different from the background) and pasting them on the background. Even small things like lines and eyes should be cut and pasted.

4. Attach a string or yarn loop to the top for hanging by:

    A. Using a hole puncher, and pulling string through

    B. Spiraling the yarn, and stapling it to the top

Front   Back.

For the Felt Option:

Use a template or pattern to cut the design out of two pieces of felt and one piece of tagboard (or light cardboard, cereal box sides). Cut the tagboard down so it is slightly smaller than the felt.

Cut all features and designs out of felt in colors different from the background. Make one piece of felt the front with a face, the other the back of the figure. Glue the features and details onto the front and back felt pieces with glue sticks or light dabs of white glue. Sandwich the tagboard between the front and back, so that it won't be seen, glue together. Make a loop with needle and thread, and hang.

Follow the same procedure for cotton stuffed figures, stitching rather than gluing front and back, leaving an opening for stuffing. Round out the figure slightly, and finish stitching.

Ideas for Follow-Up Activities

Hang completed designs on a Jesse tree. Encourage people to learn more about their symbol, what it means, and tell the story to others.

· FOR AGES 8 AND UP ·

Some first and second graders will also be able to make these, especially with parental help at home, or in a parish family event. A "how-to demonstration," as well as a "faith meanings" discussion will help.

Older children will be able to read the *Jesse Tree Chart* themselves; nine year olds can also begin to find related scripture passages. Those ten years old and up can begin to do research, and present meanings to the rest of the family, or to a class. They can also read a scripture story, or retell it in their own words for a meal prayer, or as part of an Advent prayer. You will help your children grow in faith as they become more involved with spiritually oriented Advent/Christmas crafts and activities.

Jesse Tree Chart
· THE ANCESTRY AND OLD TESTAMENT SIGNS OF JESUS ·

ANCESTOR	SYMBOL	SCRIPTURE	MEANING
ABRAHAM	Flame, Altar	Genesis 17:1-6	Father of faith, who trusted God
ADAM & EVE	Apple	Genesis 2:15-22	The happy fault that brought Jesus
BETHLEHEM	City & star Bread	Micah 5:1	City of David's and Jesus' birth house of bread; eucharist
DAVID	Crown Key Harp Star	Isaiah 62:3,11,12 Isaiah 22:22 1 Samuel 16:23 Numbers 24:17	Royal ancestry of Jesus Authority; power to open heaven's doors Joys of heaven Hope; God's leading
ELIJAH*	Fire & water Jug & bread	1 Kings 18:30-39 1 Kings 19:3-8	Represents prophets, love, wisdom Nourishing word of God
ENOCH	Cloud & feet	Genesis 5:21-24	Walked with God; assumed to heaven
ISAAC	Ram	Genesis 22:9-1-2,13	Jesus is the saving sacrifice
JACOB	Ladder/Angel	Genesis 28:12-17	Link between heaven and earth
JERUSALEM	City	Isaiah 65:17-19, 60:1-6	God's presence, promise, hope
JESSE	Root; flower	Isaiah 11:1-19	Jesus is the culmination of Jesse's line
JONAH*	Man in whale	Jonah 2:1	Jesus' resurrection prefigured
JOSEPH*	Colorful coat	Genesis 37:3,45:24	Trust and forgiveness; integrity
JUDITH	Sword	Judith 16:1-5	Courage, deliverance from evil
LAMB	Paschal lamb	Exodus 12	The sacrifice that saves from death
MANNA	Small breads	Exodus 16:13-15	Jesus is the "bread from heaven"
MARY	Rose; flower	Isaiah 11:1	The springtime of salvation
MELCHIZEDEK*	Bread; wine	Genesis 14:18,19	Prefigures mass, eucharist
METHUSELAH	Grey beard	Genesis 5:25-27	Long life, prefigures eternal life
MOSES*	Tablets Burning bush	Exodus 24:12, 16-18 Exodus 3:1-8	God teaches the people God present; holy ground; mission
NOAH	Ark; rainbow	Genesis 6:8,9:14-17	Jesus, our ark of safety; promise; hope
RUTH	Wheat sheaf	Ruth 1 & 2	Faithful ancestor by choice
SOLOMON	Temple	1 Kings 3:5-12	Wisdom and worship
SUN OF JUSTICE	Sun	Isaiah 58:6-11	Jesus' reign of justice, light
TENT	Tent; Fire	Exodus 40:34-37	God present to God's people
TEMPLE	Temple	1 Kings 8:22-23	God present to God's people

* Not an actual ancestor of Jesus, but a sign, or prefiguration of Jesus and the New Testament.

Materials and Preparation

The same as those for *Jesse Tree Symbols*.

Developing the Craft

For the mobile ornaments, needle and thread are necessary to allow figures to dangle and move freely from or within the main symbol. Thread the needle, tie a knot on one end of the thread, and pass it through the top of a figure, such as Noah or the Jesse tree flower. Then pass it through the main symbol (the whale, or the green leaf circle) and pull until the smaller figure is centered in the opening. Knot the thread again so that the figure stays in place. You may also glue the thread at both ends, and hold with scotch tape until it dries.

Many of the ornaments, such as the flower in the Jesse tree symbol, are inverted to create a three-dimensional effect. Two flowers (stars, trees) are cut halfway through, one from top to center, the other from bottom to center. Pass the two openings through each other until the centers meet, and the ends are even. Place each figure at right angles to the other, and keep in place with a dab of glue or scotch tape. For the Jesse tree flower, cut thin strips of a contrasting color, and work these through the slits, close to the center, to form stamens and pistils. Fan out between the flowers as much as possible, and dab with glue to hold.

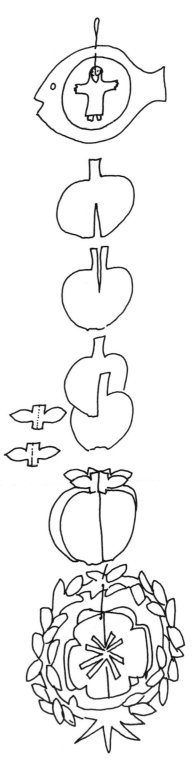

Christmas Tree Symbols

· FOR AGES FOUR AND UP ·

Materials

All those listed for *Jesse Tree Symbols* (except bare branches) plus the following options that children especially enjoy:

Glitter and white glue
Shiny and metallic papers
Small pine cones
Red ribbon, ¼" to ½" wide
Optional: Pattern copies from this chapter;
             Corrugated box lids, the kind in which reams of copy paper is delivered. Parishes and offices usually have a supply. Substitutes are other boxes, newspapers, kitchen cookie trays and aluminum foil pie plates and roasters.

Preparations

The same as that for Jesse tree symbols, with the addition of a "glitter station" that will enable you and the children to have an easy clean-up. The following steps should help:

1. Designate one area of the house/room only for the glitter part of the project. Teachers or large parish groups may also want to invite a parent or a teen "Glitter Queen" to assist at this station.

2. Cover the station area with newspaper or a large piece of plastic. If you can, find a corrugated carton, or lid with low sides, or one of the substitutes listed above. Have one for each color glitter.

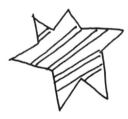

Developing the Craft

Follow all the steps outlined for Jesse tree symbols, adding a demonstration of glitter and shiny papers.

GLITTER: After a pine cone has been given a hanging loop of red ribbon or yarn, and/or after a construction paper decoration has been completed, with its hanging loop, take it to the glitter station. Instructions for the use of glitter are in the last section of the introduction to this book.

SHINY PAPER: Simply paste on decorations to add gleam and glow. Put dots, stripes, geometric shapes, or colorful clothes on any of the decorations made from patterns, or your own design.

Explain the Meanings of the Symbols

As you help children and other participants choose their Christmas tree decorations, tell them of the meanings embodied in the designs, so that their faith will grow through a happy event. Study and share the meanings presented previously. For a parish community builder, you may even want to print it up and hand it out. Adults can read it, and parents can use it at home to help their children better understand their faith, and have happy memory banks connected to their religious experience.

The *Christmas Light Reading* at the end of this chapter may be read by parents to their children to further enrich their understanding of this key Advent/Christmas sign. Turn down the lights, and read it at a meal shortly before doing the craft with them. Let the lighted candle brighten the darkened room throughout the meal, to give them an experience of darkness and light, just before they work at the craft. While they work, discuss the sign of light that is celebrated during this season. Some questions you can ask are:

1. If you were in a dark tunnel, and saw a light at the other end, how would you feel? Where would you want to run? How does light make us feel? What kinds of light are important to people, to all life on earth? What kinds do you like best?

2. What does light do for plants? Animals and us? How is light related to life on earth? Why does the Bible use light to tell us a little about who God is? Who Jesus is? Can you remember ever hearing light mentioned in church? Why did St. John say of Jesus, "He is the true light that enlightens everyone that comes into the world"?

3. Why are Christians called to be "Children of Light"? What can we do to live and act as people of light?

Ideas for Follow-Up Activities

Hang ornaments on Christmas tree, with lights and other decorations. Together, pray the *Blessing of the Christmas Tree.* Relating a prayer experience to a craft that children have enjoyed is a powerful faith-building action.

Make extra decorations to send/bring to a hospital or nursing home, senior center, soup kitchen, to cheer others. Help children learn to share their joy and love with others.

Go on to some of the more advanced mobile and sewn felt decorations that follow.

· FOR AGES 8 AND UP ·

Materials and preparation are the same as those for Christmas decorations, with the addition of the techniques described previously for *Mobile and Dimensional Jesse Tree Symbols.* Instead of reading about and explaining Jesus' ancestors, encourage children to discuss the meaning of Christian symbols of light, peace, love and joy. They may enjoy looking up related scripture passages and reading them at meal prayers, and at the *Blessing of the Christmas Tree.* Let them read the *Christmas Light Reading* and light/snuff/light the candle.

Clay-Dough Decorations

Many of the decorations and patterns described in the previous Jesse and Christmas tree symbols may be made in more permanent form from the clay-dough recipes and techniques described in the introduction. Mixing, kneading, and forming symbols is a most satisfying, relaxing, enjoyable experience to connect with your child's growth in faith. The results also make wonderful Advent and Christmas gifts, an incentive to share something meaningful and beautiful with others.

As you form your figures, it is best to keep them flat rather than trying for "sculpture in the round." They can, however, be modelled into three dimensions by building up or adding noses, hair, wings, etc., or you can simply scratch in details/features/ clothing with a wooden ka-bob skewer, nut pick, knife, long nail, or other pointy object. Textures may also be used to make more interesting ornaments.

With careful packing, these ornaments will last and continue to give their faith message for many years.

Felt Ornaments

FOR ALL AGES, AS LONG AS THEY CAN HANDLE A NEEDLE

Felt ornaments may more easily be stored and taken out over a period of years. Even young children can make them with adult help, and a large needle with a large eye, and older children will enjoy having their skills and resources challenged. They will also be involved with the faith meanings of these symbols over a longer period of time, and be reminded of them year after year, as they admire the beautiful works of their hands.

Materials

    Felt, in white and different colors
    Cotton balls, or light cotton stuffing
    Scissors
    Needles (large with big eyes, especially for children)
    Thread, white and colors to match the felts
    Optional: sequins, beads, embroidery threads, ribbons
            White or fabric glue

1. Use template or pattern to cut two pieces of felt exactly the same.
2. Sew together with a small running stitch about ¼-inch in from the edges, leaving a small opening.

TREE
SYMBOLS

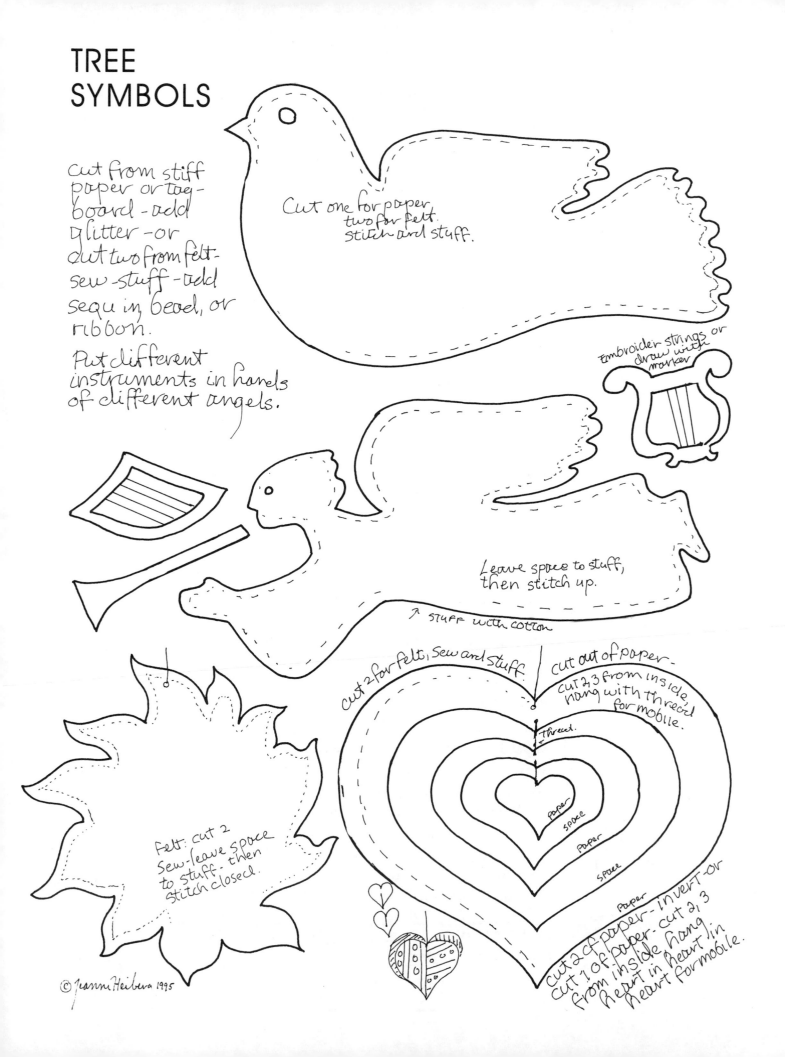

cut from stiff
paper or tag-
board - add
glitter - or
cut two from felt-
sew - stuff - add
sequin, bead, or
ribbon.

Put different
instruments in hands
of different angels.

Cut one for paper,
two for felt.
stitch and stuff.

Embroider strings or
draw with marker

Leave space to stuff,
then stitch up.

↑ stuff with cotton

cut 2 for felt, Sew and stuff.

Cut out of paper -
cut 2,3 from inside,
hang with thread
for mobile.

Thread.

paper
space
paper
space
Paper

Felt: cut 2
Sew - leave space
to stuff - then
stitch closed.

cut 2 of paper - invert - or
cut 1 of paper, cut 2,3
from inside, hang
heart in heart
heart for mobile.

Blessing
of the
Christmas Tree

God of all brightness and light, our creator,
Thank you for the gift of trees.
They fill us with a sense of life, and delight.
Trees give fruits that nourish;
Their wood builds shelter;
Their paper products pass on knowledge;
Their green and pleasant shade refreshes.
The evergreen tree reminds us of Jesus,
Who came to bring us into everlasting life
Through the tree of the cross.
In honor of his birth on earth we adorn this tree,
Whose green branches speak unending life;
Whose lights speak your shining presence in us;
Whose colors speak joys you give,
Whose stars speak your guidance,
Whose spheres speak a world renewed,
And a unity of many people made one, in peace, in God.
Let the brightness of the tree add to our joy this season,
And increase your love in our hearts,
As we awaken further to you,
And awareness of your great gifts
In Christ your son, in whom we pray. Amen.

3. Push a few fluffs of white cotton through the opening, enough to gently round out the design, and sew this up also.

4. Optional: sew on sequins, beads, or added felt pieces to form features, or decorate. You may want to add a sequin eye or several to form a collar on the dove, or give glitter to the angel's trumpet.

5. Pin a loop of yarn to the top of the ornament and hold, to see how it balances. Does it hang at the angle you wish? Correct if necessary, then sew the loop on.

A Community Building Activity

Here's a way to build parish community, give people spiritual nourishment, delight and joy, during one of the busiest times of the year. Many people would love to make decorations together, but don't have the time and materials. If a parish team (or one creative leader) gathers the materials, arranges for food and music, and invites everyone to an evening, or an after-Sunday mass get-together, they will enrich the lives (and faith) of all who come.

Issue invitations early; invite people to bring their own scissors, needles and thread if they wish, but come in any case. Have a sign-up sheet for contributions of cookies, cake and juice, or a committee that will provide them, along with coffee and tea, through phone calls or purchase. Music need only be a cassette or CD player, and recordings of Advent and Christmas music.

The materials are those previously listed for Advent and Christmas tree decorations. Run off copies of the patterns, have children you know help you make templates out of tagboard, and samples of the decorations; build up a collection. Put Jesse tree symbols on beautiful bare branches set up in a heavy jug or jar, weighted with sand if necessary. Hang Christmas decorations on a small table-top tree, with or without lights and tinsel.

Before the project, set up two or three long folding tables with a buffet of patterns, templates, construction paper, felts, yarns, cotton stuffing. Working tools such as scissors, glue, markers and crayons may also be placed here, or where people will work. Spread plastic or newspapers over their tables, or leave stacks, and ask them to spread them out, and later roll and toss them out after the work is done.

Enlist the help of other adults and teens to be on hand to show people how things work, encourage them, get needed supplies from the buffet as they work.

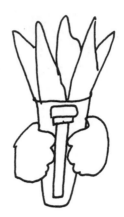

At the end of the buffet, or nearby, have a glitter table, with a "glitter princess" to assist people, especially young children. Show them how it works according to the directions in the introduction: *Frequently Used Techniques and Materials.*

At the beginning of the decorating time, give a brief explanation of tree and decorating meanings, so that participants will understand the faith dimensions of what they will be doing. Show a few of the craft possibilities, a few techniques, and let them go!

You may also arrange to have everything so well laid out, with written meanings and directions, that people can simply come in after a mass (the focal prayer), get on line, and get started.

After Class Sessions:

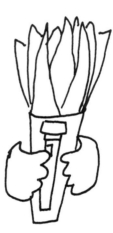

This kind of community builder is very effective in bringing together parents and children in a catechetics program, and it gives prayer the dimension of joy that it really should have.

Many non-churchgoers who simply drop off their children for religion classes each week, may have more incentive to also attend mass and other activities when, as part of a church function, they experience: a warm welcome, happy and involving crafts, music, food, community and joy.

Invite parents to come early to pick up their children, and wait in an auditorium or gym, around the outer edges.

Have children process from their classes, singing Advent songs. If possible, have each class led by a candle bearer or two. Safe substitute candles can be made by wrapping flashlights in a white or red cylinder of construction paper, with a flare of yellow construction or art tissue fluffing out from the top.

As children enter the auditorium have them form a large circle around a central Advent wreath; use masking tape, if you wish, to guide the circle. After a welcome by a leader, and perhaps a song, read a brief scripture, or the Christmas light reading given below.

For the reading on light, place the reader where everyone can see him/her, by a table with a candle, matches or lighter, and a Bible. Instruct the reader to stop and wait so that the lighting is done in complete silence, to let word and gesture each speak clearly in its own language.

Have a lighting of the Advent wreath, a song or two more, and a closing prayer; spontaneous or from the missal. Keep things brief, for the sake of the youngest children; such a prayer should be for the whole community. If you have a music or choir director who can teach songs quickly, make the most of that. Then invite everyone to make decorations, enjoy refreshments, and visit with their friends and neighbors.

Another way to pray at any decoration project, including a large community builder: Ask people to make two decorations, and put one immediately on the communal tree. Before everyone leaves, pray the *Blessing of the Christmas Tree,* by itself, or with any of the enrichments described here.

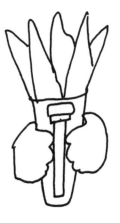

Christmas-Light Reading

Dear children, This is a holy book *(stop, hold book high)*, the book of God's word. In it we learn that God made the world, and each of us, out of love. He made us in his own image, and meant us to be full of love for him and for one another. God's love was a light in the hearts of the people he created. *(Stop, light candle in complete silence.)*

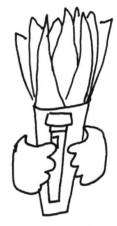

After a while, people forgot why they were made, and who made them. They began to do evil, mean things to one another, to hurt one another. The light of God's love in them was snuffed out. *(Stop, snuff out candle in complete silence.)* The world became a dark, unhappy place.

But God would not let the people he created remain in darkness. God sent his only Son, Jesus, to be born as a human being, to bring us the good news of God's love. The light came back into the world again. *(Stop, light candle, and Advent wreath candle(s) as well.)*

God invites us to open our hearts to his love, in Jesus. When we accept God's love for us, and share it with one another, the world becomes a happy place, filled with light, and we become happy too.

This is why Christmas is a time of joy and many lights. We are celebrating the birth of Jesus, who brings us back into God's light and love.

SUN STAR CHAINS

Paper link

Cut stars from construction paper.
Decorate front; write good deeds on back.

String link

© Jeanne Heiberg 1995

CROWN CHAINS

To form 3 dimentional chains,
make longer crowns. Paste
into circles. Link with paper
strips. Pass strips through 2 crowns and paste.

Sun, Star and Crown Crafts

Many crafts begin in Advent and culminate at Christmas, without leaving enough glow left over for the great feast of the Epiphany, on the Sunday closest to January 6th. The crafts in this section will help you lead up to, and celebrate Epiphany with more of the radiance it deserves.

The chain craft must be started in Advent, while the star mobiles and Epiphany crowns may be made then, or later, during the Christmas holidays, providing more fun throughout the season.

Read the brief reflections at the beginning of all three sections, whether you do them or not, so that you can reinforce meanings and motivations for those that you choose to do.

Advent to Epiphany Chains

Psychologists say that if good actions children do are recognized, there will be less need for punishing misdeeds later. Here is a creative way to not only recognize, but to celebrate good deeds in a way that will also nurture faith, hope and love.

It's an Advent tradition for children and their parents to do good things to prepare the way for Christ's coming, following St. John the Baptist's call: "Make ready the way of the Lord, make the rough ways smooth...."

Make this concrete, creative, and fun for your young people; have them cut out suns, stars or crowns — a different theme each year. Decorate them, and write on the back each Advent prayer, good deed, or loving action done to "prepare the way."

As good deed symbols accumulate, form them into chains to decorate a tree, doorway, chandelier, hallway, bulletin board, window, or other spot.

You may start this project when Advent begins, record deeds as they are done throughout the season, and put the chains together later. It is also possible to do this project close to Christmas or Epiphany from memory of things done, or from charts or lists kept during Advent. In this case, the chains can be formed at the same session.

Whether you spread this craft over the entire season, or plan one shortly before Christmas or Epiphany, you will find that the efforts of your young people deserve a ritual that adds to their significance. Blessing prayers are included here for when the family meets for a meal, or the class for instruction. You can also add them to Advent wreath prayers, blessings of crèche or Christmas tree, or Epiphany enthronements, all included in other sections of this book.

Materials

Light cardboard or oaktag
Construction paper
Magic markers and crayons
Glue sticks, glue, stapler and staples
Patterns from this book, or your own designs
Optional: Large-eyed, blunt-point needles
            Embroidery floss or thin yarn
            Shiny paper and/or glitter

Preparation

Think of ways your children can be helpful, kind, peaceable, and productive during Advent. Also think of prayers, or moments of silence and listening you would like to encourage. Prepare action and prayer ideas to discuss after you initiate the craft.

You may, if you wish, make tagboard templates of the shape you have chosen in advance, so children can easily trace around them. You can also use a paper cutter to make strips that will form the connecting links between the shapes. These may also be made by children before, or during the craft.

Initiating the Craft

Explain to children how important it is to clear our minds, hearts and lives of busy, trivial things during Advent, to focus on prayer and loving actions. It's the right time to welcome Jesus further into our lives; to prepare a bigger place inside ourselves into which God may pour gifts of love, peace and joy. More thoughts on the meaning of stars and crowns follow in the sections on mobiles and crowns.

Show the shapes that need to be cut out, to celebrate everyone's good deeds and prayers for Advent. The deed (and name — optional) goes on one side; the other side is decorated with happy colors, lines, shapes, stripes, dots, etc.

Say that you will need an abundance of suns, stars or crowns; with such wonderful children, there are sure to be many good deeds. Chores well done without complaints, scripture verses read during meal or bedtime prayers or at a class gathering, helpful actions, even a few seconds of quiet listening by young children are actions worth celebrating. (As a parent or teacher, plan to see how many times you can "catch someone doing something right" during this season.)

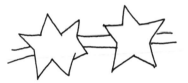

Developing the Craft

1. Choose one of the chain patterns in this section, design your own, or assign a child to this creative task. Trace the patterns onto light cardboard or tagboard and cut out to form templates. (With a small group, you may prefer to skip the template, and trace directly from the pattern.)

2. Using the template (or pattern), trace the design onto construction paper. Cut out many shapes; there are sure to be many good deeds, many prayers to write down.

3. Leave the symbols with markers and crayons (and optional shiny paper, scissors and gluesticks) in a central location. Every time someone does a good deed, they may take one, decorate the front, and on the back, write the deed (and if you wish, their name). If you use glitter, save this for a special session, or for when the chains are formed. (See glitter directions, *Frequently Used Techniques and Materials,* in the introduction to this book).

4. As decorated symbols develop, form chains as follows:

A. FLAT CHAINS: Ages 3 and up: Staple or paste strips of paper, ½-inch wide by 2½ inches long, between the suns or crowns to form chains.

B. YARN LINKS: Ages 6 and up: Make the links of thin yarn threaded onto large-eyed needles with blunted points. Space the stars, suns or crowns about 1½ inches apart.

C. FLOSS LINKS: Ages 9 and up: Make smaller symbols; use embroidery floss threaded on needles to connect the symbols.

D. ROUNDED CROWN CHAINS: Ages 8 and up: Staple both ends of a crown in back to form a round crown, decorated side out. Cut

paper strips, ½-inch wide by 9 inches long, to loop through two rounded and stapled crowns on either side to join them. Staple the connecting link. Continue to add another strip and crown on either side until you have the length you want.

Follow-Up Activities:

1. Decorate your home or classroom for Christmas or Epiphany.

2. Send chains to hospitals or nursing homes as a gift of service and love.

3. Pray one of the prayers that follow while children hold the chains. Play Christmas carols while they bring them forward to a special place (prayer or dining table), pile them in a basket, or even hang them. Add scripture readings from the lectionary or Sunday missalette if you wish.

Chain Prayers for Christmas and Epiphany

Sun or Star Prayer

Thank you Lord, for the light of your presence in our lives. Look with favor on the spiritual preparations we have made for the coming of your Son, Jesus. In your eyes, we know our deeds of love are precious and beautiful.

May our prayers and offerings create within us a greater space in which your light may shine, your love may glow, so that with Jesus we will be lights that shine in the world, for our own happiness, and that of others. We ask this in Jesus' name. Amen.

Star Prayer for Epiphany

Lord God our creator, with the gift of your Son, Jesus, you gave us hope. When you sent him into our world to help us, you called wise men to find him with the guidance of a star. Now you give each of us a star to find the presence of Jesus in our lives. Help us to live as he did, with love for you and all the people you have created. Help us to faithfully follow our star, as we grow in prayer and in care for one another. Amen.

Crown Prayer for Epiphany

Lord our God, you have given us a kind and gentle king in Jesus, who loves and serves the people he governs. He came to tell us how much you love us. He asks us to join him in helping others, and spreading the word of your love. May our prayers and loving actions help more people to know what a great and good king we have in Jesus, so that your peace, light and joy will grow in this world. We ask this as your beloved children in Jesus, our king, in whom we work, love and pray. Amen.

Epiphany Star Mobiles

"Twinkle, twinkle little star"; that song celebrates the fascination and interest that stars hold for children, and most adults. Van Gogh celebrated them in his painting, "Starry Night". His swirling worlds of light may inspire you more than the five or six pointed traditional stars, and free you and your children to express stars in your own way, as you make star mobiles. However you express them in your craft, they hold great meaning.

The wise men found Jesus by following a bright star. In those days people believed that everyone born on earth was represented by a star that appeared at the time of birth. Today's astronomers may not agree with that idea, but the kings were right in a spiritual sense. Everyone has an inner star, a light, a vision that will, if seen and followed, lead to peace, love and joy.

Our inner stars represent the seed of God's life planted in each of us when we were created. They are sparks from Jesus' own light, meant to lead us back to God, life and love. For children, the star shines in the love, guidance and promise they receive from God through their families, and from all others who help them become their best selves.

Stars represent hope and the promise of a happy future. Following your star leads you to care for others, to support life, to give in many ways, according to your gifts. It helps you overcome dark, destructive, negative forces in and around you, enabling you to become the positive, peaceful, happy, loving and creative person God meant you to be.

The world becomes a happier place for all when people follow their stars. Think what would have been lost if St. Francis, Mozart, Michelangelo, Madame Curie and Florence Nightingale had not followed theirs! Think of all the people who have overcome setbacks, handicaps, difficulties and opposition in order to achieve peace, civil rights, justice, and those things that benefit many, such as hospitals, libraries, legal systems, and democratic governments.

The precious star in each person, especially in a child, needs to be nourished and fed, for stars are vulnerable to the dark forces of hatred, bitterness, resentment, discouragement, weariness, meaningless and trivial goals. With encouragement from families and friends, however, the stars shine brightly, and guide people to great achievements.

The stars of adults may also be threatened because of the struggle to balance the practical and the dream, the mundane and the marvelous. Adults also become tired and discouraged. If, however, we help our children to follow their stars, they can help us to keep sight of ours. Children are good at stargazing. They still wonder about the big things. They remind us that our stars shine in a vast space, a place where, like the Magi, we will find Jesus.

The star crafts suggested here range from simple cutout construction paper shapes hung on a branch, or balanced in a mobile, to aluminum foil stars. The important thing is to help your children grow in faith as they work with their hands, and deepen their understanding of key symbols of the spiritual life.

· STAR MOBILES ·

Materials

    Tree branch or reeds, or thin dowels
    Construction paper
    Shiny paper
    Glue sticks and glue
    scissors and thread
    VARIATIONS: Aluminum foil
                  Crayons and glitter
                  Transparent straws, or tree branch painted white

Initiating the Craft

Show children the materials they will use, and how to use them. Encourage them to be inventive. After they understand how to proceed, you may want to initiate a discussion that will continue while work is in progress, with some questions: Do you like stars? Why? What do stars mean to you? Can stars mean dreams, promises, hope for good things? Can you think of people who followed their stars, and were happy, and helped other people to be happy? Why do you think the wise men followed the star? What did they hope for? Why is Mary sometimes called, "The Morning Star," and Jesus called "The Daystar?"

Developing the Craft

1. Cut stars out of construction paper. Invent your own designs, or use patterns included here. (Prepare light cardboard templates for a large group, if you wish.)

2. Cut out lines and shapes from shiny paper and adhere to stars, or use crayons and/or glitter to decorate.

3. Hang with thread from:

A. A beautiful branch, or

B. Reeds or thin dowels. Hang a star in different sizes, at different lengths on one reed, held horizontally. Tie a thread in the middle, so that it balances, and the reed remains horizontal. Tie the other end of the thread to a reed held higher. Tie more stars, even strings of them to this, and suspend this from one end of a longer reed. From another position on the longest reed, tie another cascade of reeds and stars, arranging them so that everything is in balance, and so that all the reeds and stars can revolve freely, creating a moving sculpture of stars.

Variation

Form your mobile of aluminum foil stars and spirals:

1. Cut 1-inch wide lengths of aluminum foil, ranging from 2½ inches to 5 inches. You will need from 5 to 11 of these, depending on the size of your mobile.

2. Cut spirals out of aluminum foil, about 3 inches in diameter, and about ¼-inch to ½-inch thick.

3. Hang these from a beautiful branch, painted white, or balance out on transparent straws, reeds, or thin dowels, to form a mobile, as described above.

Epiphany Crowns

Good friends, secure in the knowledge that they enjoyed a family relationship with God in Jesus, delighted in calling themselves "the king's kids." This has theological backing; we have a feast day, and many churches, named *Christ the King*. Christians, baptized into Christ, become brothers and sisters who share in his life with God, and, my friends concluded, his royal status as well.

They had a healthy self-esteem and, fortunately, a healthy sense that everyone else who lived on the planet was also a "king's kid arrived," or "on the way." This idea helped them to have esteem and respect for others. Making Epiphany crowns will help you to firm up these good values for the children you care about without being too preachy, pious or pedantic. Children's imaginations are often sparked by the idea of kings, queens, princes and princesses. Use this interest to deepen their faith and build healthy self-esteem and respect for others.

The feast of the Epiphany celebrates Jesus, our friend and brother, as king of all nations. The word "Epiphany" means "to manifest," to show, to reveal. The little baby boy celebrated on December 25th was shown to be God's Son, a king, when the wise men came to worship him. Not only local shepherds, but international royalty acknowledged him. His mission is to the whole world.

Three Beans, Three Crowns

To honor the day, there is a tradition of hiding three beans in a cake, or three almonds in rice pudding (from my own Scandinavian roots) for three people to find. The finders get to represent the Magi. They preside at the dinner, the party, the class — whatever the function is. Three crowns must be provided for them, and that is where a craft comes in.

Crowns for Everyone

You may also want to make crowns for everyone. This is democratic America, and an age with an increased awareness that, in Christ, we are all God's sons and daughters, and the "king's kids." A few people might have fun making crowns before the celebration, or have crown-making as part of the party. This helps even young children and brash teens to remember that we are all "the kings kids," deserving honor and respect.

Materials

> Craft paper, or construction paper, 12" × 18" preferred
> Scissors, staplers, staples, glue sticks
> Newsprint, typing or shelving paper for patterns
> Optional: Metallic wrapping or origami papers
>   Crayons and markers
>   Glitter and glue

Preparation

For a small family group, get out the supplies, and start. For larger groups or classes, cut paper strips beforehand with a paper-cutter or large shears. Cut strips 2 inches and 1 inch wide for Charlemagne and emperor's crown; from 4 inches to 6 inches for kings' crowns. The length of the wider strips should be at least 24 inches; measure the largest head to be crowned, and cut lengths a little longer. The 1 inch wide strips need only be 12 inches long, the length of 9″ × 12″ construction paper.

If you have large rolls of craft paper, you can cut the long strips in one piece. If you have only 9″ × 12″ paper, no problem. Strips can be stapled or glued together to fit around the head. Jewels and decorations will later cover up the joints.

For a large group, cut different color construction and shiny papers into smaller 3″ × 4″ squares, for jewels and decorations.

Developing the Craft

KINGS' CROWNS: Cut and/or piece together wide strips of paper, 4 inches to 6 inches deep, so that they wrap around the head to form a tall hat. Decorate as is, or cut out V shapes to form the traditional pointy crown, or rectangles for a different style. Cutting in diagonal V shapes or rectangular U shapes, making cuts deep and wide, or long and thin, gives you the opportunity to make your crown special. Make it even more so by cutting out jewels and decorations from different colors, or from shiny papers, and gluing them onto your crown. You can even make a solid crown with no cuts interesting, beautiful and royal, by gluing on stripes, Vs, Us, jewels and other shapes. Such variations can also be done with art tissue, crayons, glitter, and or colored markers.

CHARLEMAGNE CROWNS: Let the leader of the ancient Holy Roman Empire inspire you to make a Romanesque crown. Fit a 2-inch strip around your head, and staple or glue it together to form your crown base.

Staple the end of a 1″ × 12″ strip to the top of this shape. Pass it over the crown to the opposite side, and staple, to form an arch. Do the same with a second strip, at an equal distance from the first strip, so that both cross over the top at right angles. Attach a small cross or other symbol at the top, and proceed to decorate with colored and shiny papers, crayons, markers, or glitter.

EMPEROR'S CROWN: Form a Charlemagne crown, without the cross at the top. Add four 1″ × 12″ strips, attaching one end to the base over the shorter strips. Bring all four of the opposite ends down over

the top of the crown (where the original strips cross), so that they each curve out beyond the previous strips in an "emperor's curve." Staple these where the original strips cross. Now you can add a cross or symbol at the top, and decorative jewels all over.

Variations

1. Experiment with your own way of making crowns.

2. For a shorter time span, decorate with markers and crayons and/or glitter.

3. Form crowns out of light cardboard or poster board. Decorate as described, or cover the entire crown with fabric or felt, and decorate with brightly colored felts, bright metallic braids, trims, buttons, and/or beads.

Follow-Up Activities

1. Have an Epiphany party or dinner with three beans or almonds in one of the dishes, to determine the three kings. Have crowns for them or, if you wish, crowns for everyone.

2. Move the three king crèche figures right up to the manger scene to join Jesus and Mary.

3. Make crowns at the party or dinner, and have a crown parade to the music of "We Three Kings."

4. Have everyone write on a slip of paper the gift of love and service they want to give, to build up God's kingdom during the coming year. Collect these in a basket, and leave them as part of the manger scene.

5. Say prayers from the Epiphany Enthronement, in the chapter on Christmas crèches.

Christmas Crèches

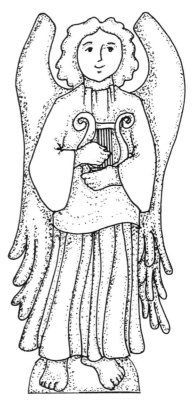

The crèche is a beloved custom that helps keep vivid the real reason for the great midwinter holiday. They have been set up in churches since the time of St. Francis of Assisi, who wanted everyone, including those who couldn't read, to know how much God loved them.

Besides celebrating the birth of a very special child, the crèche celebrates the holiness of a family going through difficulties, trusting, making the best of circumstances, finding their way, in order to protect and bring forth new life. Family and spiritual values are so strongly supported in the nativity scene, that every home should have one.

The Christmas story is understandable to even the youngest children, because most have had experiences of mothers, fathers, people who work, babies, and animals. They may not have seen angels, but children have an innate spiritual sense, and respond to the idea of heavenly messengers. The Christmas story is also about love, and you can draw on (and increase) their experiences in this area as well. Whether or not you buy a crèche made by professional artists, do have the fun and joy of making one with your children. Give them the opportunity to express their love for Jesus, and prepare for his coming at Christmas.

A variety of techniques follow, so that you can choose those best for your family's age range and available time. There are quick and easy versions for parents on the run and catechists with limited class time. However, many of you will want to work with something that will engage minds, hearts and hands in the spirit of Christmas a little longer, or that will provide a greater challenge for older children. Three-dimensional, in-the-round figures of paper, papier-mâché, bread dough, clay and fabric are for you.

Plan snacks, play Christmas music, read the Christmas story from a children's Bible during the work time to make it a faith-building experience that will be remembered with a warm glow.

Remember, as you plan the craft, that Leo Tolstoy said, "If you want to get an idea across, wrap it up in a person." The people of the Christmas story embody important ideas, values, and inspirations which will help your family members deepen their faith. If you discuss some of these meanings as you help your child(ren) make the figures, they will never forget them.

Here are some mini-portraits of the figures you will want to include in your crèche, to help you with such sharing.

Saint Joseph, a Model for Men

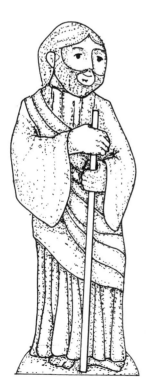

St. Joseph is the archetype of the father/protector, the worker who takes care of the family. Even though the town of Bethlehem was crowded, and housing unavailable, he didn't give up until he found a safe place for Mary. Then he creatively made the best of the stable so that she and her new baby would be comfortable. He loved Mary and Jesus, worked hard to earn a living for them, and was alert to defend them from all danger.

Men, women, and children need to have a little of St. Joseph inside. Even the youngest members of the family have pets, toys, rooms to take care of, and at times, people around them that need help. St. Joseph can inspire older children, who have increasing responsibilities, to work with care and craftsmanship.

St. Joseph is often pictured with carpenter's tools; however, in a crèche, he sometimes carries a staff, an instrument of protection and support. He both protected and supported the Holy Family, and through prayer, allowed God to protect and support him. Alert and attentive to God, he allowed himself to be guided by angels that visited him in dreams and prayer. He was not too busy, as many are today, to heed angels, and so he received support and strength to be a model man and head of the family.

Men and boys need to be encouraged to learn how to be guided by God, so that they become successful family and community leaders. Many need to learn to protect those less strong, and develop skills to take care of those who will some day rely on them. Masculine gifts of strength and skill are needed in families, churches and communities; however, men, and all of us, need to remember that true strength lies in prayer, gentleness, and kindness, with openness to God and angels.

Mary the Mother

While Mary is most often shown sitting with the child on her lap or kneeling by the manger, early depictions showed her lying down, a more realistic posture. A family crèche may also show her standing with St. Joseph, the manger between them, in a symbolic, rather than a realistic way.

The seated figure of Mary holding Jesus, often called "The Madonna," is one of the most celebrated and revered signs in art. It images the deep archetype of motherhood, the wonder of new life, the beauty of love as a reflection of God. The Madonna reminds us that we all need mothering, nurturing, love, and we are all called to nurture and love others. What Mary did before Jesus was conceived, her response to God's invitation, makes her a model, showing us how to proceed.

Because Mary said "yes" to God, Christ could be born into the world, to bring us all back to God. Like Mary, we all need to say our own "yes" to God, so Christ can be born in our hearts and lives, in love. We also need to help others say their "yes" so that Christ can be born in them.

Every Christian, whether man or woman, boy or girl, has a mothering, nurturing task to bring forth Jesus' new life in ourselves, others, and the world. The more people who say "yes" to God, and let God's love live in them, and guide them, the more this world becomes like heaven, a happy and peace-filled place.

Mary was able to be fruitful and creative in partnership with God because she was humble, and aligned her will with God's, rather than trying for the reverse. She was willing to be the least among people, and so God was able to make of her the greatest among women.

The Child Jesus

Jesus came to awaken us to who we really are, sons and daughters of God, as he is. Humanity was created in God's own image, with the very attributes of God, such as love, kindness, generosity, strength, peace, joy, and light.

Sadly, humanity separated from God, and allowed darkness, fear, sin and guilt to overshadow these gifts. Like the prodigal son, the human race forgot it had a parent who deeply loves each son and daughter, and who wants to share peace, love, joy, light, and all good things with everyone.

That's why Jesus came, as one of us, with a wake-up call: "This is who you really are, a child of God, greatly beloved, called to share God's life and love with me, and in me."

Coming as an infant, Jesus demonstrated who we are in relation to God — a child, totally dependant on a loving parent who gives us everything. We all have an *inner child* with deep longings for our true home, heaven, and our great parent, God. We keep this inner child peaceful and happy by allowing him/her to "go home" to God every day, when we are quiet in prayer for even just a few minutes. Advent is a special time to remember and practice a holy silence, a "going home."

The birth of God's Son as an infant also tells us that God values *being over doing,* important as good actions are. As a baby, Jesus was an embodiment of life and love, unable to accomplish anything practical, yet God's precious child, prince of the kingdom, celebrated by angels and kings.

You may want to make a crown for the infant for the feast of the Epiphany, or even a more royal child to replace the Christmas infant (see Kings, below).

Shepherds

In Jesus' time, shepherds represented the lowest strata of society. That they were called to Jesus first, even before the highest strata, the kings, arrived tells us that everyone is called to God's kingdom of peace, love and joy. God's gifts are for all. To further this idea, add shepherdesses to your crèche. They will represent half of humanity, whose members do a lot of the menial, hard work of the world.

Shepherds were, like St. Joseph, protectors, caretakers, of life. Jesus later called himself the Good Shepherd, who would even give his life for his sheep, us, the children of God. The call of the shepherds shows us how much God values those who work humbly and hard to watch over, feed, care for, and protect life.

Angels

God's messengers/helpers, the angels, are not sentimental, cute or weak, but ardent, awesome, and of great power. Invisible spirits, they have often appeared to people in familiar forms, to help God's people on their journey home.

The Bible often describes angels as beautiful young men in white robes, shining with light, sometimes with wings, a sign of spiritual soaring and heavenly freedom. The book of Revelation pictures angels awesomely, with faces like the sun, circled in stars, one foot on land, and the other in the sea. There are no wimpy angels in scripture.

In art, angels sometimes play musical instruments, appropriate for those who praised God at Jesus' birth. Giving praise and glory to God, rejoicing in God's love, protecting humans and carrying messages all fall under their job description. Recent books on angels say they are quick and eager to protect and aid us, but we have to invite them. Prayer opens windows from their world into ours so they are able to come to our rescue, and help us in reaching our goals.

It's good for children to know they have powerful protectors assigned by God to take care of them. Speak of this as they make them for the crèche. Encourage your children to form kind, but strong angels that express the power of beings mighty in love to do what God needs done.

Once a part of your Christmas nativity scene, they will help convey the joy of Jesus' coming, and the peace, love and happiness God wants us to have in his beloved Son.

Kings

The kings, Magi, or wise men, represent the highest of humanity bowing down before a far greater, though infant dignitary, bringing their most precious tangible gifts in order to receive the far greater, though intangible gifts of God.

The royal travelers represent all nations, all peoples coming to worship Jesus. God's Son is for everyone, regardless of race, religion, nationality, tribe, age, sex, talent, handicap, financial or social status. No one is excluded unless they exclude themselves.

To demonstrate this inclusiveness, it's a great tradition to show the kings as three different races and/or nationalities. Their adoration establishes Jesus as spiritual king of all human beings, inviting everyone to recognize their sonship/daughtership in God.

The kings traditionally carry gifts of gold, frankincense (in a censor) and myrrh. If your figures carry these, they will dovetail with the verses of "We Three Kings," and the prayers of the Epiphany enthronement ritual at the end of this chapter.

Besides making three kings for your crèche, you may also want to make a more kingly Jesus-child, to place in the crèche on the feast of the Epiphany, the Sunday closest to January 6th. This is a way to celebrate Jesus' manifestation as king of all creation. Let one of your children place this kingly child in the manger or in Mary's arms, as a way for everyone to say, "Jesus, I want you to be my king, too."

You In the Crèche

Some crib sets include modern figures, such as a boy and girl, and possibly a few adults. You may want to include your family; your children may want to include themselves in the nativity scene. It is a wonderful way to express a wish to welcome and adore the baby Jesus; to say that you want to live by the values and teachings of Jesus, and be part of God's kingdom of peace, love, light and joy. This is the kind of concrete prayer that young children need to nourish their life of faith.

Animals

It is well-known that Jesus, the royal prince of heaven, allowed himself to be born in a stable to show his love for all of us, including the most poor, humble and lowly. I believe there is also another reason: children love animals. Go to the library, and see how many well-loved children's books include them! Jesus must have known this, and allowed himself to be surrounded by beasts at his birth so that children would find even greater delight in making and setting up crèches.

Traditionally, the doves symbolize peace, the ox strength, the donkey humility, and the sheep obedience to God, all delightful options to include in your set. Feel free to also let your family pets and favorite animals form part of the group celebrating Jesus' birth. In these times when much of the earth's life forms are threatened, we need this reminder: all creation is renewed and saved as God's children remember who they are, and what they are called to do. This includes caring for and protecting life in all its rich and varied forms.

Paper Craft Crèches

Paper craft crèches are the easiest to make, the most inexpensive, possible for all who are able to wield a crayon, marker, or cut, paste and glue. The techniques that follow range in time from 10 to 20 minutes up to an hour and more for 9 to 12 year olds, who often become absorbed in doing beautiful dimensional figures.

Initiate the craft by showing the techniques, and also by talking about each character needed in the set. When spiritual meanings are prominent in young, forming minds as they enjoy creative work, their faith is deepened.

Quick and Easy Crèches

· AGES THREE AND UP ·

Materials

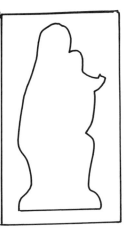

Copies of figures from this chapter
Light cardboard (tagboard, posterboard, cereal or soap box sides)
Crayons and/or magic markers and pencils
Scissors, glue sticks, and scotch tape
Optional: Colored construction paper
          Templates that you have cut from tagboard

Preparation

Make enlarged copies of figures from one of the pattern pages, or use them as a pattern to cut out templates from tag (or other) board. If you give your children just the outline, they will be able to draw in their own faces and clothes; this is the preferred, more creative option. You also have the choice of giving them copies of drawings, so that children need only color and cut.

Older children may enjoy cutting features and clothes out of different colored construction paper, and gluing them on the background. Have paper ready for them in a variety of sizes — 9″ × 12″ sheets cut into halves, quarters, plus scraps.

Developing the Craft

1. Use a tagboard template, or a cutout figure from one of the pattern page copies, to trace an outline onto white or light colored construction paper.

2. Cut out identical figures from both the paper and light tagboard. If you use copies from a pattern page, roughly cut out the figure, place it on the tagboard, and cut out both shapes at once, following the outline of the figure.

3. Lightly rub a glue stick over the front of the tagboard, and the back of the paper. Place the paper carefully on the tagboard, and press lightly to smooth the surface. When the surface is smooth, place another sheet over the figure, and firmly press with your hand, or roll over it with a pencil (on its side) to fasten firmly.

4. Draw in features, hair and clothing, or color in the features that are already there. For those who work in construction paper, cut and paste every part of the design to form your figure.

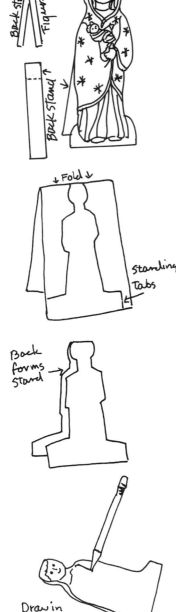

Back stand. Figure.

Back stand?

↓ Fold ↓

Standing Tabs

Back forms Stand

Draw in features and clothes.

5. Cut stand-up tabs out of tagboard, and crease 1 inch down from the top.

6. Hold the top of the tab on the back of the figure while you spread the bottom at an angle. Move the top tab until you find the angle at which the figure stands upright, then draw a light pencil outline around the top and sides on the back of the figure. Fasten the tab top only at that point, with glue stick and/or scotch tape. Do not stand again until the glue is dry.

VARIATIONS: A-LINE, FOAM BOARD AND FLANNEL BOARD

A-Line (quick and easy)

1. Fold a piece of light construction paper the long way. Place the top (head) of the template or pattern up against the fold.

2. Hold a ruler against the bottom, below the feet, and draw a straight horizontal line that extends 1½ inches on either side of the figure's edge.

3. Measure ¾-inch up and draw a parallel line that also extends 1½ inches from the figure's edge, then draw two vertical lines at the outside ends to join them.

4. Cut around the outside of the figure and its base, taking care not to cut the top, where the fold is. The front and back must remain joined at the top.

5. Draw in features, hair and clothes with a magic marker, or cut and paste different color construction paper to add these.

6. Spread the front and back bases apart so that the figures will stand to form your crèche.

Foam Board (challenging)

Instead of tagboard for the backing, use the light foam board that backs up meat and other products in your grocery store. Wash it well before use, and follow directions for developing the craft for flat figures.

Older children who work carefully can use thicker foam board from a craft or office supply store as a backing. They will need a good exacto knife for this kind of work.

Follow directions for developing the craft for flat figures; however, instead of a cardboard tab on the back, glue one or two small squares of the foam board on the back of the figure so that it will stand. These

EASY TO MAKE CRÈCHE

© Jeanne Heiberg 1995

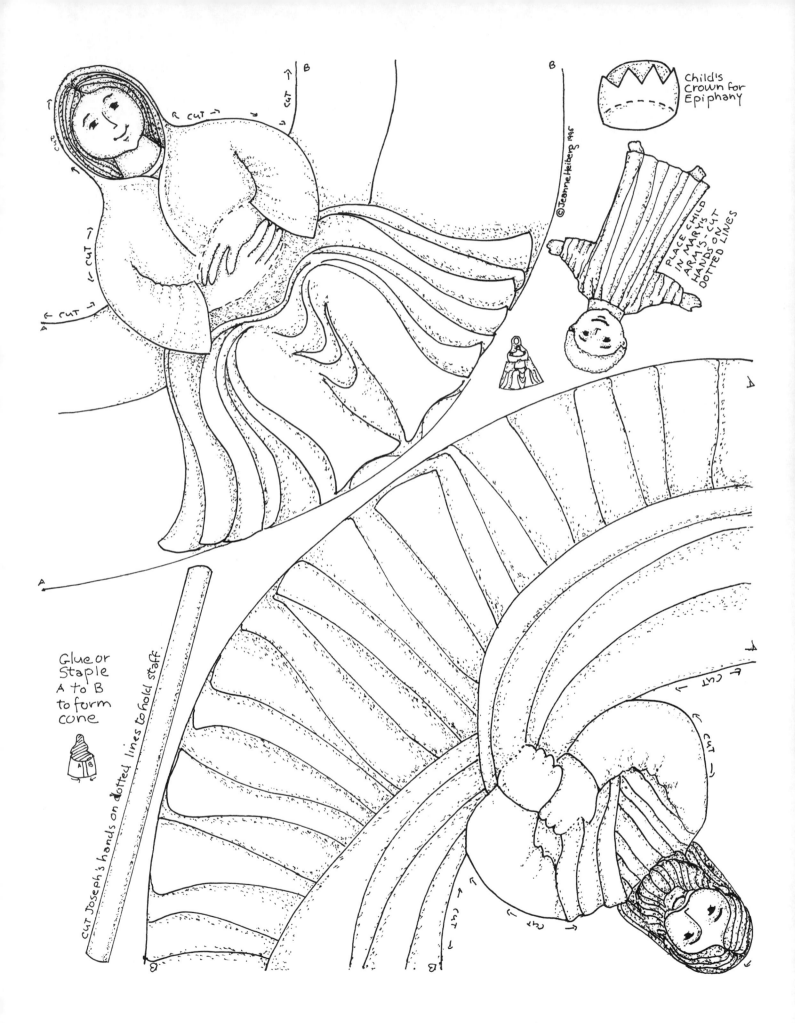

Child's Crown for Epiphany

©Jeanne Heiberg 1996

PLACE CHILD IN MARY'S ARMS - CUT HANDS ON DOTTED LINES

Glue or Staple A to B to form cone

Cut Joseph's hands on dotted lines to hold staff.

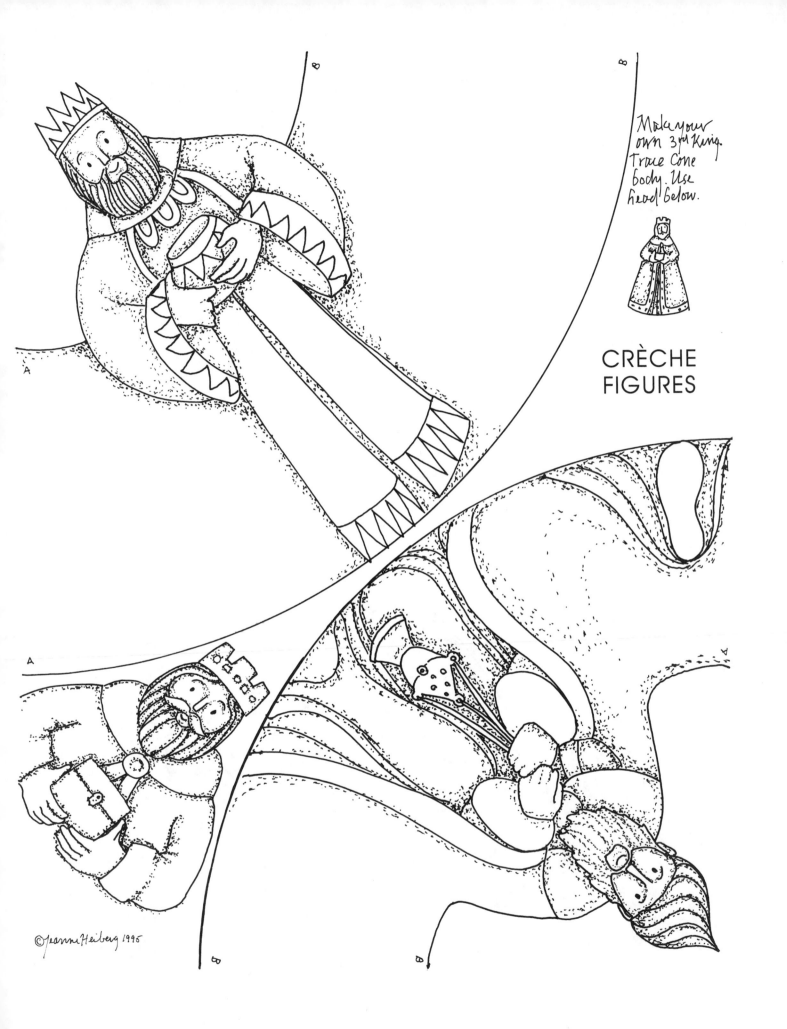

Make your
own 3rd King.
Trace Cone
body. Use
head below.

CRÈCHE
FIGURES

©Jeanne Heiberg 1995

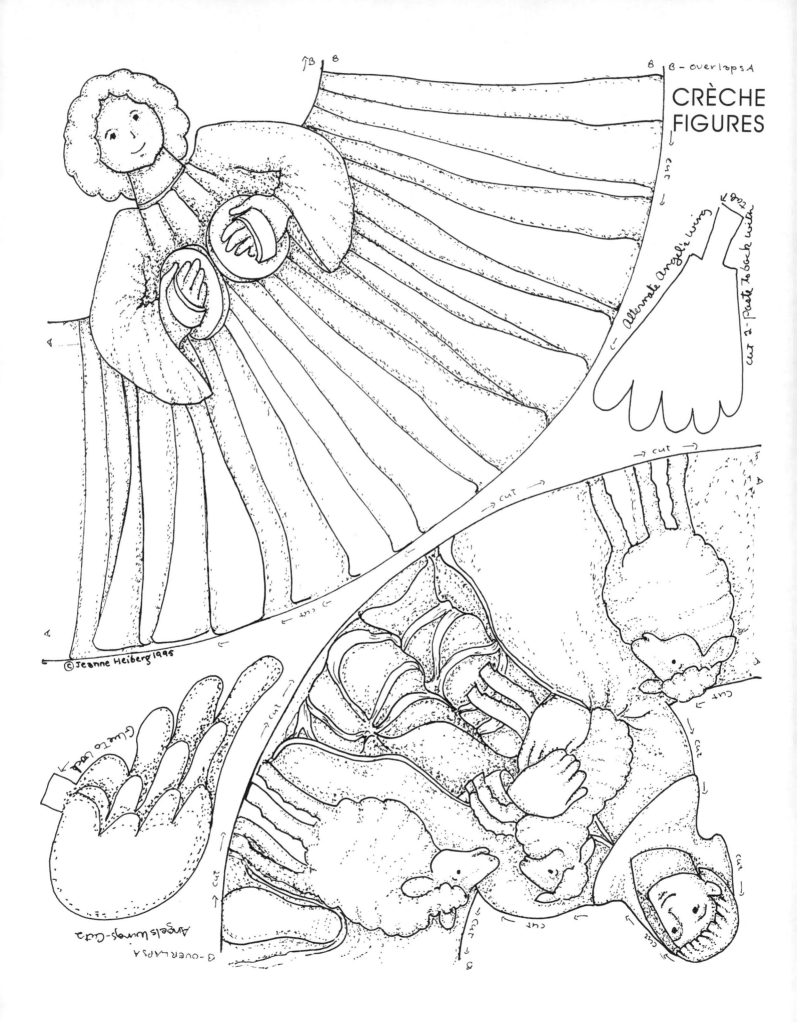

CRÈCHE
FIGURES

© Jeanne Heiberg 1995

figures give a little more sense of dimension, something 10 and 11 year olds (and parents) can look on with pride.

Flannel Board

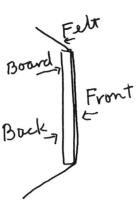

If you back up your paper figures with felt or flannel, instead of tagboard, and make a background on which to place them, you have a flannel board. You can add, take away, and move the figures as you tell young children, 2 to 6 years old, the Christmas story. You can also invite them to pick up and place the figures at the appropriate times in the story.

To make the backboard, you will need a large piece of heavy or corrugated cardboard or plywood, from 18″ × 20″ up to 24″ × 36″, and a piece of felt large enough to cover it, plus at least 3 inches all around. Choose a color that will make a good background: black, deep purple or blue, for Christmas night (though white and green are also possible).

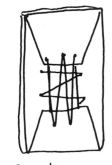

Wrap the extra material around the edges of the cardboard, so that they flap over to the back. Pull it taut so that the material is smooth over the front of the backboard, and hold it in place at the back with masking or scotch tape. Use a needle and thread or glue to fix it more firmly, and your background is ready for storytelling.

For the figures, use the instructions for developing the craft, substituting felt or flannel for the cardboard and, of course, leave out the stand-up tabs.

An advantage of flannel board: when you tell the story, your angels can fly in the sky, and you can easily add the star and scenery — trees, bushes, cave or stable, some lines for mountains and hills. The more pieces, the more involved your child will be in a beautiful faith-building activity.

In-the-Round Crèches

· AGES 6 AND UP ·

As children grow older, they need to embody their ideas in interesting materials and craft techniques. When a quick, expressive, primitive drawing no longer satisfies, forming features out of cut paper based on geometric shapes, or modeling with papier-mâché, claydough, and fabric will give them a sense of achievement. Involving them in deeper meanings of the figures in the crèche will give them the

spiritual, as well as the craft challenges they need to grow in faith at this stage, so that meanings will inspire faith as well as craft.

Cylinders (AGES 6 AND UP)
Cones (AGES 8 AND UP)

Materials

Multicolored construction paper
Glue sticks, glue and scotch tape
Scissors, staplers and staples
Optional: color swatches from magazines; fadeless art paper or origami paper; art tissue.

Preparation

Review the *Frequently Used Techniques and Materials* section from the introduction, so that you can demonstrate ways of working with paper. Decide on whether you want the human figures in your crèche to be based on cylinders (easier for younger children) or cones (just a little more challenging). Read over the Christmas people meanings above, so that you can discuss faith meanings of the figures.

Developing the Craft

Form a sheet of the construction paper into a tall cylinder, or into a cone, and staple. Continue to follow the directions given in the last section of the introduction. Figures in this chapter will give you further ideas for making arms, cloaks, faces and beards; use them as patterns, or create your own.

Papier-Mâché

Two, three, even four sessions will be needed for this craft, with time in between to allow figures and paint to dry.

Materials

Newspaper, at least 15 sheets per figure
Art paste, wheat paste or flour

One large plastic container for mixing
Optional smaller containers, one to every two or three people
White/multicolored tempera or acrylic paint
Brushes, water and paper towels
Masking and scotch tape, string, glue and scissors
Plastic to protect working surfaces.

Preparation

With a paper cutter or scissors, cut ⅓ of the newspapers into strips about ½-inch wide. Mix the papier-mâché paste in a large container such as a plastic bucket or dish pan. For a larger group of children, divide this into smaller containers (pound margarine, butter containers or coffee cans), to distribute. Everyone should have easy access to these, and they can be refilled as needed.

Decide on the height you want your figures to be; prepare an armature of that size as a model. Don't worry about art; this is for measuring only.

Optional: precut sheets of newspaper to the sizes needed for heads (both the crumpled base and the covering sheet), arms and body; this will give a unity to the crèche figures. You or an older child may even precut sheets 4–5 layers thick, rounding off the part that will form the base, so that cones of a similar size may be more easily formed.

Developing the Craft

1. Crumple a sheet of newspaper into a ball the proper size for a head. Take a smooth, fresh sheet and wrap it around the front and top, gathering the loose ends at the bottom. Work with the cover and wad to form a slightly projecting chin, and a smooth face. Fasten with string or masking tape.

2. Take three or four layers of clean newspaper and wrap them around the loose ends of the head, overlapping to form a cone wide enough at the base to stand. Fasten with masking tape.

3. Starting at the shortest point, trim the base so that all of it is equal to where you started. Fasten firmly. Crumple up more newspaper, and stuff inside the cone. Hold this in place with masking tape across the bottom.

4. Roll a shorter section of newspaper layers into a thinner cylinder and fasten. Find the middle point, and place on the middle of the figure's back. Bend the arms around to the front, and fasten with string and/or tape. Work with the arms further, to place them in a position you like for that figure.

5. Follow the steps and patterns in cone and cylinder figures to add capes, wings, hair, crowns, gifts, musical instruments. Fasten with glue, string and tape as needed. Roll up a thin cylinder to form Joseph's staff, or use a dowel or pencil. Form animals from cylinders as described in cylinder figures; newspapers are easier to shape into body, neck and head, than construction paper.

6. When the armature shape is as you wish, begin to cover and strengthen it by dipping strips of newspaper into the paste, and smoothing over the figure. Work different parts of the figure so that drying can take place before the next layer. If you alternate black and white strips with color strips from the comic section, you can keep track. Cover the figure with four layers, then allow to dry thoroughly.

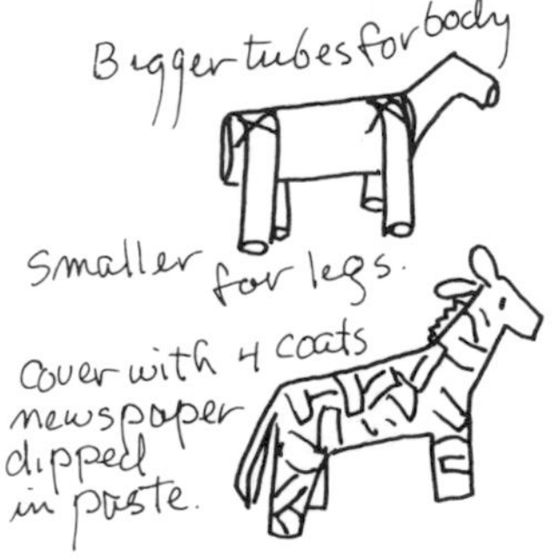

7. When the figure is thoroughly dry, cover with a coat of white tempera paint, and allow to dry.

8. Paint skin color, features, hair, clothes and other details on the figure with colored tempera paints.

VARIATIONS:
BOTTLES, SOAKED NEWSPAPER, AND FABRIC

Bottles:

Use bottles, rather than newspaper cones as the base for the armature. Make the head as described, stuff the ends inside the bottle neck, then proceed as above.

Papier-Mâché Mash:

See recipe and directions in *Frequently Used Techniques and Materials* in the introduction.

Fabric:

A. Build armatures with paper cones or bottles, then use fabric for clothes, wool for hair, found objects for gifts. Use fabric in different textures, weights, colors for contrast.

B. Use a fine cotton fabric, dipped in heavy starch, before you drape it over the armature. This allows you to control the form and flow, and create a unity among all the figures. The fabric has interesting qualities in itself, so junior high and high school students find satisfaction and a sense of achievement in the craft.

all kinds of wings!

different instruments!

Bigger tubes for body

smaller for legs.

Cover with 4 coats newspaper dipped in paste.

Bottle based figures

Bottle Based Figures. 12-16 oz bottles work well.

dip cloth in heavy starch for elegant clothing - shape as you wish!

Clay-Dough Crèches

Small figures may be modelled in the round, if care is taken that no part of the figure is more than double in thickness to any other part. Use aluminum foil to build up an armature around which you work the figures. That will keep the sides thin, and support the dough until it air dries, or bakes. Oven bake only, if you use the metal foil.

For recipes and further directions, see *Frequently Used Techniques and Materials* in the introduction.

Felt Puppets

Felt Puppets. Patterns are on page 80

stitch yarn for hair pack tight

2 strands of yarn for mustache

Roll arms for sleeves; sew.

Slip arms between front and back panels.

Materials

Copies from the pattern page
White, pink, beige or brown felt or other fabric
Felt/fabric in colors for clothes, crowns, wings, capes.
Yarn, excelsior or sphagnum moss for hair
Sand or rice and cotton stuffing
Scissors, pins, needles and thread in colors to match cloth.
Optional: embroidery floss or thin wool yarns
needles with wide eyes

Development of the Craft:

1. Copy and cut out basic figure shapes from the pattern copies, extending the bottom, if necessary, so that the entire figure will cover the bottle. Use to cut figures out of felt.

2. Form the figures as described on the patterns, and in the diagrams. Test arms to be sure you can fit your thumb and middle finger into the sleeves. Glue or stitch on capes and other clothes.

3. Add yarns for hair. Cut a length twice as long as you wish the hair to be. Stitch to the head at the center; pack strands closely together for a full, vibrant effect. Stitch yarn beards on Joseph and the kings. Add crowns for the kings, dowel staff for St. Joseph and a halo for the baby Jesus.

4. Place figures over bottles to form a crèche. Pick them up, slip your index finger into the head, thumb and middle finger into the arms, to activate the puppet during story time.

Follow-Up Activities

Background and Stable

The figures from any of the methods described may be placed on a table or under the tree as they are, though you will probably want to cushion the infant with straw, excelsior, sphagnum moss, cotton or material. Find a small box, or make one from a milk carton covered with paper or felt to hold any of the softeners.

You can also make a felt background ranging from a simple star-spangled sky to a scene with hills, trees, cave or stable. Elements of the scene may be glued or stitched onto the background.

Girls and boys often like to build things, and making a stable out of twigs, balsa wood, popsicle sticks, driftwood or lumber scraps can provide a great challenge.

Storytelling

Tell the Christmas story, moving the figures or puppets as you do, or invite children to bring up each figure and place it in the scene, or on the board, at the proper time. When they know the story, let children tell it and move the figures.

Ritual and Blessing

Set the crèche up during Advent, omitting the infant, and placing the kings at a distance, in another part of the room or house. Let young children place something — a straw, a puff of cotton where the infant will later rest, whenever they do a helpful action or kind deed, or say a prayer. The good things they do will make a softer cradle for the baby Jesus, a sign of welcome.

On Christmas eve, have a short prayer time during which the figure of the Christ Child is carried in procession, and placed in the manger, or on the straw.

During the Christmas season, move the kings up periodically, timing their journey so they will arrive close to (but not quite up to) the crèche on the feast of the Epiphany, the Sunday closest to January 6th. On this day, have a short prayer of enthronement. If you have made a more regal Christ Child, place him in the crèche at this time. If not, make a crown for the head of the infant and, if you wish, Mary and Joseph.

Blessing the Crib

Have ready a cassette or CD player with favorite carols. Those presented here are ideas you may replace with those your group knows and likes. Encourage everyone to sing along.

(Gather everyone around the crèche, and play/sing "O Little Town of Bethlehem").

LEADER: Loving God, our creator, you call us out of darkness to be children of light, peace, and love, in Jesus your Son. You sent him to be with us, to teach us how much you love us, and to bring us back into your light.

Bless this crèche *(extend hand and make sign of cross toward crèche, then people)*, and all who gather around it. Let it be a sign of joy to us in this season as we celebrate the coming of Jesus, in whom we pray. Amen.

CHILD: *Places the baby Jesus figure in the manger or on the straw.*

(Play/sing "Away in a Manger," or another appropriate carol.)

LEADER: May this crib keep alive in us the awareness of your love, and that of Jesus. May it open our minds and hearts further to the mystery of your Son, born humbly in a stable. Let us also live humbly, love tenderly, and walk always in your ways.

(Play and sing "Silent Night," "Joy to the World," "O Come All Ye Faithful," and other favorite carols.)

Epiphany Enthronement

Preparation

If you have a royal child figure, remove the Christmas infant before the prayer begins. If you do not, leave the infant, and have a crown ready to place on its head. Have a cassette or CD player ready with Christmas carols. "We Three Kings," "O Come All Ye Faithful," and "Joy to the World" are good choices.

Options:

Make crowns for all who will be present at the prayer (see *Epiphany Crowns*), in the preceding chapter. Have them ready, in a basket or box, to place on people's heads at the appropriate time, indicated in the prayer.

Add the placing of crown, sun or star chains made during Advent. (See the preceding chapter.)

The Prayer

LEADER: Blessed are you, great holy God, king of the universe. In your love for us, you sent your Son to be our king, to bring us back to you as sons and daughters, members of your own royal family.

CHILD: *Places royal Jesus in the crèche, or crown on the head of the Christmas infant.*

LEADER: Loving God, you called wise men to honor your Son, Jesus, leading them by the light of a star. May we also respond to your light in our life, and follow the inner stars, the love sparks you light in our minds and hearts, that bring us closer to you, Jesus, and one another.

CHILD: *Moves the king carrying gold up into the crèche.*

LEADER: With the gift of gold, we praise Jesus as your royal Son, who came to lead us into your kingdom of love. Help us to be aware that, as brothers and sisters of Jesus, we are royal as well. Help us to treat one another royally, with kindness and respect. Help us to share our resources and riches, the good things you give us, to help one another and to share the joy of your love.

CHILD: *Moves king carrying censer up into the crèche.*

LEADER: With the gift of incense, we praise Jesus as true God, come to help us know the divine life you give to each of us. Help us to forgive and see beyond mistakes, as we look for that spark of divine life, your presence, in ourselves and others. May we be faithful in prayer, remembering to talk to you each day, so that we will always grow in your love.

CHILD: *Moves king carrying myhrr up into the crèche.*

LEADER: With the gift of myhrr, we celebrate Jesus as truly human, come to be like us and with us in all but sin and mistakes. He opens up the way for us to return to you, sharing help, love and happiness as we go. Because of Jesus, even the difficulties and hard things of life are easier, and bring us closer to you. We know that you are always with us, loving us and helping us.

LEADER: Jesus, our king, calls you to share his royalty, and to join him in bringing God's peace, light and love into our families, schools, and places of work. It begins in our own hearts and minds, and grows as we share it with others. Take a few quiet moments now, to rest in God's peace and love. Listen to God's word in your heart, to see if there is a message for you of sharing, of helping, of caring for those around you. (*For older children and adults, add that* God helps us to make a difference. May we work with Jesus to extend peace and justice in our world, knowing that our happiness will grow as God's love grows in us and others.)

RITUAL ACTION
(Going to each person, the leader or other adult(s) places a crown on the head, OR their hands on the head or shoulders of each person, saying:)
LEADER: " (Name of Person) ", you are God's own royal child, called to live in God's peace, love, and joy.
           (For older children able to grasp concepts of justice and service, you might choose another affirmation after their name, such as: "You are a royal brother/sister of Jesus, invited to help him expand God's reign of justice and love.")
(Play a tape or CD quietly during this ritual.)

CLOSING PRAYER
LEADER: Jesus, we acknowledge you as king. May the peace and love you came to establish be rooted firmly in us, and shared with others in our family, school, and workplace. We pray that your kingdom of love will grow among all the peoples of the earth, and that we will make a difference through our daily prayers and actions. Amen.

(End with "Joy to the World," "Joy is the Flag," "King of Kings," "The King of Glory Comes," or a favorite of your own.)

FELT PUPPETS

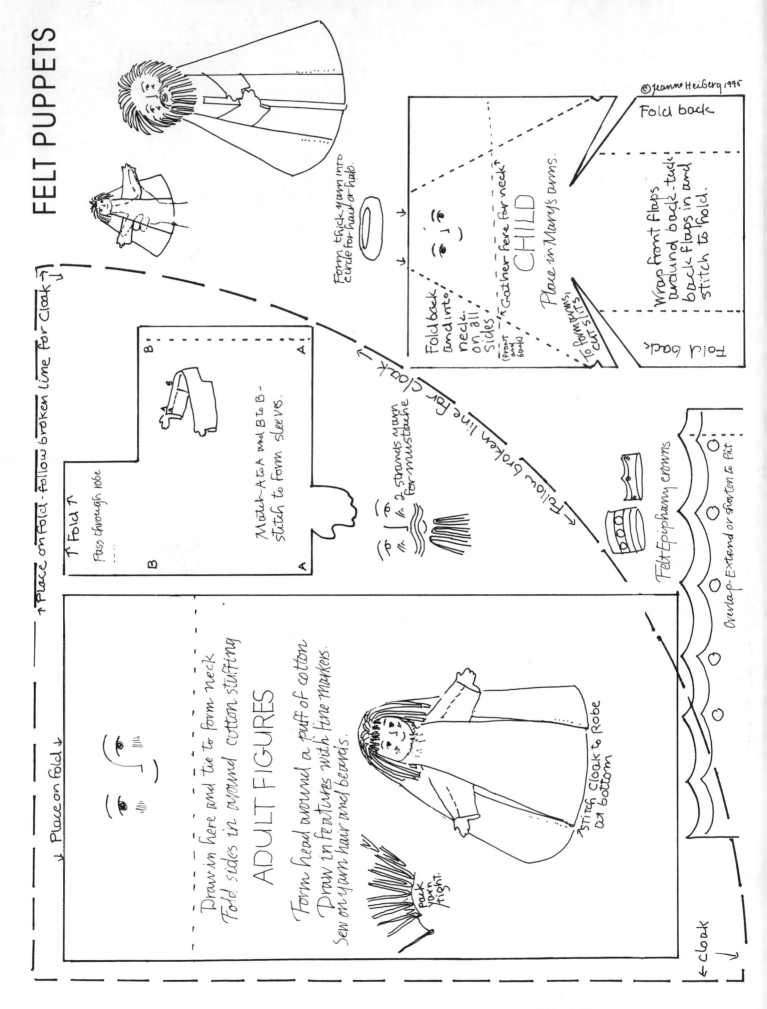

© Jeanne Heiberg 1995

Fold back

Wrap front flaps around back, tuck back flaps in and stitch to hold.

Fold back

Fold back and into neck on all sides

(Front and back)

← Gather here for neck ↑

CHILD

Place in Mary's arms.

To form arms, cut slits

Form thick yarn into circle for hair or halo.

← Place on fold - follow broken line for cloak ↑

↑ Fold ↑

Pass through robe

B .... A

B   A

Match A to A and B to B - stitch to form sleeves.

← Follow broken line for cloak →

In 2 strands yarn for moustache

Felt Epiphany crowns

Overlap-Extend or shorten to fit.

↑ Place on fold ↓

Draw in here and tie to form neck
Fold sides in around cotton stuffing

ADULT FIGURES

Form head around a puff of cotton
Draw in features with fine markers.
Sew on yarn hair and beards.

pack yarn tight.

Stitch Cloak to Robe at bottom

← cloak ↓